MEDEA

Medea, the sorceress of Greek myth and Euripides' vengeful heroine, is famed for the murder of her children after she is banished from her own family and displaced by a new wife. Her reputation as a wronged 'everywoman' of Greek tragedy has helped engender her lasting appeal to the modern age. However, this firmly rooted status has also caused many of the intricacies of her timeless tale to be overlooked.

Emma Griffiths brings into focus previously unexplored themes of the Medea myth, along with providing an incisive introduction to the story and its history. Viewed within its context, the tale reveals fascinating insights into ancient Greece and its ideology, the importance of children, the role of women, and the position of the outsider and barbarian.

The critically sophisticated analysis, expressed in clear and accessible terms, proceeds to examine the persistence of the Medea myth through ancient Rome to the modern day. Placing the myth within a modern context and into analytical frameworks such as psychoanalysis, Griffiths highlights Medea's position in current classical study, as well as her lasting appeal. A vivid portrait of a woman empowered by her exclusion from society, alive with passion and the suffering of wounded love, this book is an indispensable guide to a fascinating mythical figure.

Emma Griffiths is Lecturer in Classics at the University of Manchester.

MEDEA

Emma Griffiths

Routledge
Taylor & Francis Group

LONDON AND NEW YORK

First published 2006
by Routledge
2 Park Square, Milton Park, Abingdon, Oxon OX14 4RN

Simultaneously published in the USA and Canada
by Routledge
270 Madison Avenue, New York, NY 10016

Routledge is an imprint of the Taylor & Francis Group

© 2006 Emma Griffiths

Typeset in Utopia by Keystroke, Jacaranda Lodge, Wolverhampton
Printed and bound in Great Britain by TJ International Ltd, Padstow,
Cornwall

British Library Cataloguing in Publication Data
A catalogue record for this book is available from the British Library

Library of Congress Cataloging in Publication Data
A catalog record for this book has been requested

ISBN 10: 0–415–30069–X (hbk)
ISBN 10: 0–415–30070–3 (pbk)
ISBN 13: 978–0–415–30069–8 (hbk)
ISBN 13: 978–0–415–30070–4 (pbk)

CONTENTS

SERIES FOREWORD

For a person who is about to embark on any serious discourse or task, it is proper to begin first with the gods.

(Demosthenes, *Letters* 1.1)

WHY GODS AND HEROES?

The gods and heroes of classical antiquity are part of our culture. Many function as sources of creative inspiration for poets, novelists, artists, composers, filmmakers and designers. Greek tragedy's enduring appeal has ensured an ongoing familiarity with its protagonists' experiences and sufferings, while the choice of Minerva as the logo of one of the newest British universities, the University of Lincoln, demonstrates the ancient gods' continued emblematic potential. Even the world of management has used them as representatives of different styles: Zeus and the 'club' culture for example, and Apollo and the 'role' culture: see C. Handy, *The Gods of Management: who they are, how they work and why they fail* (London, 1978).

This series is concerned with how and why these figures continue to fascinate and intrigue. But it has another aim too, namely to explore their strangeness. The familiarity of the gods and heroes risks obscuring a vital difference between modern meanings and ancient functions and purpose. With certain exceptions, people today do not worship them, yet to the Greeks and Romans they were real beings in a system comprising literally hundreds of divine powers. These range from the major gods, each of whom was worshipped in many guises via their epithets or 'surnames', to the heroes – deceased individuals associated with local communities – to other figures such as daimons and nymphs. The landscape was dotted with sanctuaries, while natural features such as mountains, trees and rivers were thought to be inhabited by religious beings. Studying ancient paganism involves finding strategies to comprehend a world where everything was, in the often quoted words of Thales, 'full of gods'.

In order to get to grips with this world, it is necessary to set aside our preconceptions of the divine, shaped as they are in large part by Christianised notions of a transcendent, omnipotent God who is morally good. The Greeks and Romans worshipped numerous beings, both male and female, who looked, behaved and suffered like humans, but who, as immortals, were not bound by the human condition. Far from being omnipotent, each had limited powers: even the sovereign, Zeus/Jupiter, shared control of the universe with his brothers Poseidon/Neptune (the sea) and Hades/Pluto (the underworld). Lacking a creed or anything like an organised church, ancient paganism was open to continual reinterpretation, with the result that we should not expect to find figures with a uniform essence. It is common to begin accounts of the pantheon with a list of the major gods and their function(s) (Hephaistos/Vulcan: craft; Aphrodite/Venus: love; and Artemis/Diana: the hunt and so on), but few are this straightforward. Aphrodite, for example, is much more than the goddess of love, vital though that function is. Her epithets include *Hetaira* ('courtesan') and *Porne* ('prostitute'), but also attest roles as varied as patron of the citizen body (*Pandemos*: 'of all the people') and protectress of seafaring (*Euploia, Pontia, Limenia*).

Recognising this diversity, the series consists not of biographies of each god or hero (though such have been attempted in the past), but of investigations into their multifaceted aspects within the complex world of ancient paganism. Its approach has been shaped partly in response to two distinctive patterns in previous research. Until the middle of the twentieth century, scholarship largely took the form of studies of individual gods and heroes. Many works presented a detailed appraisal of such issues as each figure's origins, myth and cult; these include L.R. Farnell's examination of major deities in his *Cults of the Greek States* (5 vols, Oxford, 1896–1909) and A.B. Cook's huge three-volume *Zeus* (Cambridge, 1914–40). Others applied theoretical developments to the study of gods and heroes, notably (and in the closest existing works to a uniform series) K. Kerényi in his investigations of gods as Jungian archetypes, including *Prometheus: archetypal image of human existence* (English trans. London 1963) and *Dionysos: archetypal image of the indestructable life* (English trans. London 1976).

In contrast, under the influence of French structuralism, the later part of the century saw a deliberate shift away from research into particular gods and heroes towards an investigation of the system of which they were part. Fuelled by a conviction that the study of isolated gods could not do justice to the dynamics of ancient religion, the pantheon came to be represented as a logical and coherent network in which the various powers were systematically opposed to one another. In a classic study by J.-P. Vernant, for example, the Greek concept of space was shown to be consecrated through the opposition between Hestia (goddess of the hearth – fixed space) and Hermes (messenger and traveller god – moveable space: Vernant, *Myth and Thought Among the Greeks*, London, 1983, 127–75). The gods as individual entities were far from neglected however, as may be exemplified by the works by Vernant, and his colleague M. Detienne, on particular deities including Artemis, Dionysos and Apollo: see, most recently, Detienne's *Apollon, le couteau en main: une approche expérimentale du polythéisme grec* (Paris, 1998).

In a sense, this series is seeking a middle ground. While approaching its subjects as unique (if diverse) individuals, it pays attention to their significance as powers within the collectivity of religious beings. *Gods and Heroes of the Ancient World* sheds new light on many of the most important religious beings of classical antiquity; it also provides a route into understanding Greek and Roman polytheism in the twenty-first century.

The series is intended to interest the general reader as well as being geared to the needs of students in a wide range of fields from Greek and Roman religion and mythology, classical literature and anthropology, to Renaissance literature and cultural studies. Each book presents an authoritative, accessible and refreshing account of its subject via three main sections. The introduction brings out what it is about the god or hero that merits particular attention. This is followed by a central section which introduces key themes and ideas, including (to varying degrees) origins, myth, cult and representations in literature and art. Recognising that the heritage of myth is a crucial factor in its continued appeal, the reception of each figure since antiquity forms the subject of the third part of the book. The volumes include illustrations of each god/hero and where appropriate time charts, family trees and maps. An annotated bibliography synthesises past research and indicates useful follow-up reading.

For convenience, the masculine terms 'gods' and 'heroes' have been selected for the series title, although (and with an apology for the male-dominated language), the choice partly reflects ancient usage in that the Greek *theos* ('god') is used of goddesses too. For convenience and consistency, Greek spellings are used for ancient names, except for famous Latinised exceptions, and BC/AD has been selected rather than BCE/CE.

I am indebted to Catherine Bousfield, the editorial assistant until 2004, who (literally) dreamt up the series and whose thoroughness and motivation brought it close to its launch. The hard work and efficiency of her successor, Matthew Gibbons, has overseen its progress to publication, and the classics editor of Routledge, Richard Stoneman, has provided support and expertise throughout. The anonymous readers for each proposal gave frank and helpful advice, while the authors' commitment to advancing scholarship while producing accessible accounts of their designated subjects has made it a pleasure to work with them.

Susan Deacy, Roehampton University, June 2005

ACKNOWLEDGEMENTS

I gratefully acknowledge the permission of the following institutions to reproduce the images in this volume: Figure 1, supplied copyright Trustees of the British Museum; Figure 2, supplied copyright the Cleveland Museum of Art; Figure 4, supplied by the Bridgeman Library of Art; Figure 5, supplied by the Library of Congress; Figure 6, image supplied copyright Bayerische Staatsgemäldesammlungen, Neue Pinakothek Munich.

My thanks are due to the series editors, Susan Deacy, Catherine Bousfield and Matthew Gibbons, for their patient and perceptive support. My friends, colleagues and students at the University of Manchester have been a constant source of ideas and encouragement while writing this volume, and my greatest debt of thanks is due to my family.

ILLUSTRATIONS

WHY MEDEA?

1

INTRODUCING MEDEA

Why should we care about a mythological figure who uses magic, kills children and is never punished? Is there something we can identify with? Does it matter that the mythological figure is a woman rather than a man?

One reason for this book is simply the fact that Medea still has a presence in modern society. Unlike figures of Greek myth who would be unfamiliar to most modern readers (does anyone remember Psamathe or Rhadymanthos?), the name Medea still holds a place in the modern imagination. (This volume will use the common form of her name, rather than the more literal transliteration from the Greek as 'Medeia'.)[1] We might suggest that her name remains in memory only because plays about her have survived, but even the subjects of surviving ancient plays, such as Hekabe or Thyestes, receive little attention outside classical circles. Medea, on the other hand, is known by those who have never read a Greek tragedy; the subject of art throughout the western tradition, she has been used as a figurehead by political movements, and her name is frequently mentioned when society confronts an act of infanticide, even though Greek myth tells of several other child-killers, such as Prokne or Ino. The name Medea means 'The Planner', and it may be her strategic powers which have caused her to be singled out for sustained attention.

Medea is not an obviously sympathetic figure for modern audiences. Her abilities and actions make her an unlikely focus for identification or the glamorisation which can attach to figures such as Herakles or Achilles. If we consider her fascination as part of a gendered dialogue, focusing on powerful women, there are other figures of Greek myth who would equally deserve attention: Klytaimestra, who murders her husband Agamemnon, the story immortalised in Homer's *Odyssey* and in the most famous of Greek tragedies, Aeschylus' *Agamemnon*; Eriphyle, an ancient gold-digger who betrayed her husband for the sake of a necklace; the Amazons, warrior women who rode out to battle and famously invaded the city of Athens. This cast of powerful women all have affinities with Medea, but it is she who has remained pre-eminent.

This book has two interrelated aims. First, it will give readers an understanding of the background which is implied when modern artists speak of 'Medea' – the narrative framework, the origins and the meaning(s) to ancient cultures. Secondly, it will explore the myth and the source of its power – why the story of this one figure inspired so much attention in the ancient world, and how it has retained its popularity in the modern world.

THE UNIVERSALITY OF MYTH

It is remarkable that the myths of ancient Greece are still current after more than two millennia of use, playing a role in a range of societies with divergent interests. How, then, do these myths survive? The ancient world can be seen to underpin western society, and ideas of cultural authority outlined by Seznec (1953) will be relevant to our discussions of the 'afterlife' of the myth in Chapters 8 and 9, where we will see the spread of the Medea myth as a global phenomenon. A further reason for the continued popularity of Greek myth is that of universality. The key idea, that human nature remains constant and that Greek myths speak to that core humanity, can be formulated in many ways. We can look to the psychoanalytical idea expressed by Jung that there are archetypes in the collective unconscious: Jung believed that we all inherit a mental set of patterns which we use to create our own place in the world, assigning roles to ourselves and to others from a limited number of 'archetypes'. The mental pattern book is the same across different cultures and periods of history, which is why, Jung believed, we are able to relate to ancient cultures as to our own. A complementary approach is the anthropological stance associated particularly with the nineteenth-century theorist Andrew Lang, which argues that all human cultures progress via the same stages, so that similar motifs develop independently. When we look at a Greek tragedy or a Roman poem it is often easy to apply these stories to our own lives, ignoring the details and focusing on emotions or fundamental human concerns, such as family or love. However, this line of argument is deceptive, particularly when we are considering a figure as complex as Medea, so a few words of caution are in order.

The principle of universality stems from a set of ideas developed in the nineteenth century, when the idea of universality was popular in many fields. Many of the central ideas have been challenged by later intellectual developments. We will be looking at a number of approaches which could be termed 'universalising' as we proceed through the discussions, but it is as well to note some of the principal objections which could be raised.

The opposing view to universal theories comes from the idea of cultural and social constructs. Instead of positing a universal human nature, the idea of constructs emphasises the degrees of interaction between individuals and groups which can create new patterns of meaning. This principle can be taken further. Some have argued that even things which we might assume to be universal, such as the experience of the physical body, are subject to a process of cultural mediation. We may all experience the same biological phenomena, but the ways in which we understand and deal with the process are determined by society. For example, women's bodies have often been treated as inherently imperfect – the Hippocratic approach to women is well discussed by King (1998), and can be seen even today in the loaded term 'hysteria', a madness associated with having a uterus. Medea's action in killing her children places her at the centre of a complex web of ideas about the female body and the relationship of children to their mother, ideas which have social and political implications.

The idea of constructs warns us to be wary when we think we can transfer ideas or images from one culture to another. A striking example of this approach to mythology comes from Freud's use of the Oidipous myth. The famous play by Sophocles was, for its original fifth-century Greek audience, not so much a play about psychological trauma as about the inevitability of fate. A story can have different meanings in two different contexts.[2] The story of a woman who kills her children can be variously interpreted depending on how a society understands the idea of 'woman', 'killing', 'children', etc. When we look back at a figure from ancient myth, there is a tendency to fill in the blanks and make a coherent picture based on our own beliefs and assumptions. In doing so we may create a false picture of Medea which tells us only about our own individual interests.

LAYERS OF MYTH

There was no canonical version of the story of Medea, and when we talk of myth, we are implying three different levels of story. First, there is the all-encompassing 'Greek myth', which comprises all the stories. Medea is involved in this wider context with many links to other figures – she is part of a nexus of stories, about Jason, Herakles, Theseus, Dionysos and others, which situates her in a complex set of relationships. Her partnership with Jason is central to both their stories, but the interactions with other figures contain much of interest. She is said to have restored Herakles' sanity after he killed his sons, linking the two infanticides. Her attempt to kill Theseus when he arrives in Athens makes her part of father/son dynamics as well as stepmother stories, and incidentally links to Herakles again: Theseus will offer sanctuary to the child-killer Herakles, just as his father Aigeus offered sanctuary to Medea. The wider context of Greek myth will be central to our analysis of the figure of Medea. A second level of 'myth' is the collection of her stories, 'the myth of Medea', a story made up of incidents told in different ways in different time periods. It is a story which overlaps with the stories of other mythological figures, and which can contain contradictory elements, such as the details of how her children were killed at her hand, or by accident, or by the people of Korinth. Finally, there are the specific 'instantiations' of the myth, that is to say the individual tellings of all, or part, of the story of Medea. The connection between the different layers of myth is complicated, and we should remember that works of art or literature which shape the material according to their own particular ends were seldom designed to give any comprehensive overview of the myth.

However, we are relatively well provided with information about Medea. She appears as the central figure in many ancient narratives and is also referred to in the stories of other major figures. Drawing upon the full range of sources we can construct a mythic biography for Medea. The major episodes are described most fully below, but the less well-attested, or less central, episodes and variants will also be discussed in later chapters.

MYTHIC BIOGRAPHY

1. The Golden Fleece. Medea is a native of Kolchis on the edge of the Black Sea, a region which was identified by the Greek world as on the fringes of civilised society. As the daughter of King Aietes, Medea is the granddaughter of Helios, the sun god, and niece to Kirke, the sorceress famed in Homer's *Odyssey*. Medea's mythical life is generally activated by the arrival of Jason and the Argonauts when they come to Kolchis to capture the Golden Fleece. Jason has been set this seemingly impossible task by his uncle Pelias, who is attempting to prevent the young heir from taking the throne in Iolkos. Medea falls in love with Jason and uses her magical powers to help him overcome the obstacles which Aietes puts before him. She leaves Kolchis with Jason, and kills her own brother Apsyrtos in the process. During the journey home, Medea causes the death of Talos, a bronze giant who threatens the Argonauts.

2. Medea comes to Greece as Jason's wife and uses her powers to rejuvenate Aison, Jason's father. There are also references to Medea rejuvenating Jason himself.

3. In Iolkos, Medea causes the death of Pelias, either on her own initiative or at Jason's request as he attempts to secure his position (there are no accounts which show Jason succeeding in gaining the throne of Iolkos). Medea demonstrates to Pelias' daughters (the Peliades) how she can rejuvenate the old, by killing an old ram which then emerges from her cauldron as a much younger

animal. Inspired by this, the daughters decide to procure the same anti-ageing treatment for their father, and proceed to kill him. Medea fails to perform the trick for the old man, who thus remains dead. Medea and Jason are forced to flee.

4.   The story moves to Korinth, where Medea, Jason and their children find sanctuary. The most famous narrative resumes when Jason marries the princess of Korinth, who is sometimes called Glauke or Kreousa. Outraged by this betrayal, Medea causes the death of the princess and exacts terrible revenge on Jason by killing her own children, leaving Jason childless. This is the famous version told by Euripides, but other variants of the myth give different reasons for the death of Medea's children which do not make her a deliberate child-killer. In some accounts Jason is the ruler of Korinth and Medea his consort, or Medea herself is the legitimate ruler. In the Euripidean version, Medea then flees from Korinth and goes to Athens.

5.   Medea is offered refuge in Athens by King Aigeus, who marries her in some versions of the story. When Aigeus' illegitimate son, Theseus, arrives in Athens Medea attempts to poison him, but Aigeus recognises his son at the last minute and dashes the poison cup away. Medea may also have tried to set Theseus an impossible task to perform. After Theseus and Aigeus are reunited, Medea flees from Athens.

6.   The final chain in the story involves one of a number of geographical moves. Medea may go to the East, where her son Medus/Medios/Medeios becomes the founder of the Medes. There are also accounts which make Medea return to Kolchis. Her final resting place is said to be Elysion, the paradise afterlife, where she becomes the wife of Achilles.

The outline given above indicates the wealth of material which comprises 'the myth of Medea', and provides some pointers as to the recurrent themes and emphases: the use of magic, the repeated escapes, the connections with fathers and children, and the fact that at no point is there any direct punishment for her actions. However, this outline conflates many different sources and episodes and blurs some of the problems and contradictions contained within the myth.

The range of contradictions has created a lively set of scholarly debates, with disagreements over the origins of Medea's story. It has been suggested that there were two original Medeas, and there are many competing interpretations about individual details or variants which draw upon, and feed back into, broader debates about the main focus or meaning of the myth as a whole.

This book will outline the main areas for discussion with guidelines on the main critical positions. The next chapter will begin with discussion of the nature of our sources, then Chapters 3 to 5 will proceed to examine key aspects of the myth, beginning with the question of origins. Chapter 6 will consider a particular moment in the evolution of the myth which may well have changed the course of its development, and the following chapter will look at how the Greek story moved into the Roman world. The final two chapters look at the reception of the story of Medea after the decline of Roman power, concluding with a snapshot of the role of Medea in the modern imagination. The fluid nature of Greek myth makes neat schematisation an impossible task (although some ancient writers such as Apollodoros attempted it!), and the figure of Medea is particularly frustrating in this respect. Although this book is intended to provide a workable structure for readers to access the main information, there will be some overlap between different sections, and readers should be prepared to crossreference different parts of the argument in order to gain a better appreciation of the material. Ultimately, the myth of Medea may contain a lesson in living with chaos. In order to appreciate the essence of this mythological figure we must abandon the comfortable illusions of certainty and academic systematisation, and be willing to entertain ways of thinking which are more relaxed and mythological.

GENEALOGICAL TABLE

Medea is usually presented as the daughter of Aietes and Iduia (also called Eidyuia or Neaira), but the family tree can then be constructed with a number of variants both up and down. The commonest ancestry makes Aietes and Kirke the children of Helios, the sun god, and Perses, an Oceanid. Aietes and Iduia are the parents of Medea and her sister Chalkiope, while Apsyrtos is fathered by Aietes from his union with the nymph Asterodeia. However, the family tree given by Diodorus Siculus (4. 45 ff.) makes Aietes and Perses the children of Helios, then makes Perses the direct ancestor of Hekate, while Aietes is father of Medea and Kirke.

Moving down the family tree, Medea's children by Jason are variously numbered, named and gendered (anywhere from one son, to seven sons and seven daughters). Euripides gives us two unnamed sons, whereas Pausanias 2.3.9 reports the account of Kinaethon (fr. 2) referring to a daughter, Eriopis, and a son, Medeios. This son, the ancestor of the Medes, is sometimes called Medos, and is sometimes said to be the child of Medea and Aigeus.

Most common genealogy

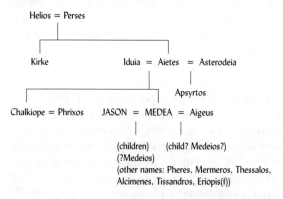

Alternative table

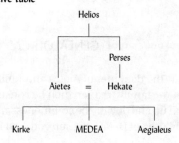

2

MYTHOLOGY AND SOURCES

This chapter will explain how we know what we know. Wider discussion of the significance(s) of Medea can only proceed from a clear understanding of the basis of our enquiry. Unlike analysis of a character in a novel, the exploration of a mythological figure is based on shifting sands. If we say 'Medea killed her children', we need to be aware that this is only one version of the myth (as told at a particular time, by a particular figure, for a particular purpose). We must also remember that this version is contradicted by other stories explaining the fate of children. The aim of this chapter is not to establish a definitive account of the myth, or to say 'this is the best source', but rather to indicate the nature of the materials we are working with.

In chapters 3 to 5 we will be examining the myth of Medea from different angles, trying to create a multidimensional picture. In constructing our mythic biography of Medea we inevitably conflate ideas, times and places, and may inadvertently gloss over issues. The next section, therefore, will examine the myth synoptically, eliciting the central problems and foci of the mythology. To do this, we will need to draw upon information from a wide range of different sources, time periods and geographical locations. We face the dilemma of the group members who each feel one part of an elephant, and declare it individually to be a horse, a snake and a rat. This chapter will provide a brief outline of the main generic considerations when using each type of source. We will also note points which are relevant for our understanding of the myth of Medea. Ancient sources for mythology can be as biased and contradictory as any modern newspaper, so we have no access to a 'pure' form of the myth of Medea, if one ever existed.

The malleability of myth, and the various ways in which it is manipulated, inevitably invite analysis of how one version builds on earlier ones. While it is not the intention of this volume to present a detailed account of the chronological development of the myth, we will note the ways in which ancient sources referred back to previous ones, both deliberately innovating and deferring to the authority of older versions. Although the obvious model would seem to be one in which the myth becomes richer as later versions build on previous ones, this is not the only temporal framework which we should consider. There is not an unbroken line along which the myth develops, and older versions can be lost or distorted. The focus of this volume will be the *ancient* idea of Medea, because her strength as a figure is derived from the power of ancient storytelling. Nevertheless, some would argue that it is impossible for us to look back to an ancient Medea, because we are unavoidably conditioned by all the later images which stand between us and the ancient sources.

There are two schools of thought implicated in this issue. The one, persuasively articulated by Sourvinou-Inwood (1991, 1995), argues that we can get close to an understanding of the original ancient world if we collect enough information to construct 'perceptual filters'. By applying these 'filters', as if putting on a pair of glasses, we can look back into the ancient world, and recreate ancient responses to the figure of Medea. This approach, sometimes referred to as working with a 'cultural encyclopaedia', is central to much of the work traditionally undertaken in the field of classical studies.

The opposing view, from a more recent, post-structuralist perspective, argues that it is impossible to escape our own mental framework. This view, espoused by Martindale (1993, 1997) and others, favours an approach which emphasises the reception history of the ancient world. By gaining a greater awareness of the distance which stands between us and the ancient world we become more self-conscious about our own roles in creating history. Viewed from such a perspective, ancient mythology is not something fixed which influences later cultures. Rather, there is a dynamic process of interaction between the two, whereby modern ideas and constructs affect our ability to access the ancient world, and thus change the ancient mythology. So modern ideas about Medea colour our understanding of ancient sources. This is an approach which can be applied to all aspects of the ancient world, including history, but it is particularly apposite when studying mythology which is inherently malleable.

This volume will attempt to steer a path between these two approaches, providing detailed context about the ancient versions, while also indicating the two-way processes by which individuals and societies come to make stories meaningful.

THE TRANSMISSION OF MYTH: ORALITY AND LITERACY

The fluidity of myth in the Greek world is related to the conditions of its creation and transmission. Although today we only have access to ancient mythology via written (i.e. literate) storytelling and through visual images, the primary medium for the evolution of mythology in the Greek world was the spoken word. The earliest Greek literature, the Homeric epics, came from a tradition of oral storytelling, where a bard composed a story afresh for each new occasion, albeit using well-known building blocks, such as story shapes or certain repeated phrases. There was a culture of performance which rewarded innovation, militating against the formation of any canonical version of a particular myth. Furthermore, this oral form of storytelling was accessible to all, regardless of education or even gender, for the mythology of popular culture was transmitted by women as much as by men, as Plato talks of 'old women's tales' (*Theaetetus* 176 b 7).

There was no clear dividing line between 'myth' and 'history'. *Muthos* meant 'a story told', and it was generally understood that events related in myths were actual reflections of historical events from a time when men were greater and the world a more magical place. We should be careful when thinking of myths in terms of allegory or symbolism: for the Greek audience there was often a far more direct correlation between 'then' and 'now' which was not necessarily mediated by any awareness of myth as a fictional construct. The fear of Medea as a real person would be more concrete than a fear of allegorised 'female power' or 'invasion from outside'. Similarly, the relationship between myth and ritual was more highly charged than we might imagine. Today we tend to talk of myths as *aetiologies*, explanatory stories, as if they were clearly fabrications, but for the Greeks who performed the rituals, belief in the historicity of the events related could be a fundamental aspect of their relationship with the divine.

There are good detailed accounts of the evidence for the myth of Medea which collate the sources and the different variants, which are detailed in the Guide to Further Reading. This section does not aim to be comprehensive, but rather to indicate the challenges we face when using these sources and the reasons why some material may be more interesting than others.

SOURCES: ARCHAIC LITERATURE

The Homeric epic poems, the *Iliad* and *Odyssey*, can with reason be called the foundation of Greek, and, by extension, western, literature. Not only are they the earliest surviving verbal art forms from Greece, but Homer was central to the education and cultural development of many Greek societies. Unfortunately, for our purposes, there is no mention of Medea in these two poems. We can, however, say with some certainty that the story of Medea was part of the repertoire of the earliest storytellers. From fragments and references in later writers we know of a range of epic poems which existed at the same time as the Homeric epics were composed. These narratives, known collectively as the 'Epic Cycle', told stories which were part of the same world of myth, with details of events before, during and after the Trojan War. Because of their origins in the traditions of oral storytelling, these poems are the closest we can get to any 'authentic' mythology. However, even the travelling poets who told these stories would have delivered them with a particular purpose in mind, be it to flatter a certain audience or powerful patron or to demonstrate poetic skill in working with the material. We must, therefore, beware of thinking of our earliest references to Medea as necessarily straightforward and without bias.

The *Nostoi* (*Homecomings*), an epic poem from the seventh or sixth century BC, told the stories of the heroes returning to Greece from Troy, and referred to Medea's powers of rejuvenation. One fragment refers to her rejuvenation of Jason's father, Aison, by placing drugs in a golden bowl (fr. 7, *PEG* = *Poetae Epici Graecae*, ed. Bernabé (1987)). Magical powers were central to the earliest stories we can access, and these powers are at the far end of the spectrum of Greek magics. Rejuvenation is a skill which indicates Medea's divine ancestry and carries with it dark associations of the underworld, as we will discuss further in Chapter 4.

From the same period (c. 700 BC) comes Hesiod's extant poem, *Theogony*. This is a catalogue of mythical family trees which tells how Jason took Medea from Aietes, and that they had a child called Medeios (vv. 922–1022). There is no mention of Medea herself taking any action. This is a poem where the overall framework of creating genealogical patterns is foremost, and Hesiod may have shaped the myths to suit his poetic purpose. The story of Jason and Medea comes in a section dealing with marriages between mortals and immortals, which strongly suggests that Medea is regarded as a goddess. The narrative also contains a perplexing statement that because of the marriage of Jason and Medea, 'Zeus' intention was fulfilled'; the meaning of this phrase is uncertain, but West (1966) notes it as a reference to the destiny of Medea's child, Medeios, possibly linked to his founding of the Median race (see further Chapter 5).

The earliest surviving reference which gives Medea a central role in capturing the Golden Fleece comes from the late seventh-century BC poet Mimnermus (fr. 11a), who says that Jason would not have won the fleece without 'her' help. The text does not make clear that the female in question is Medea, and there is an alternative tradition which makes Athena the principal source of help, but the context strongly suggests that there is a relationship between Jason and his helper beyond that of a mortal to an Olympian goddess. Although Mimnermus does not elaborate on the reasons for Medea's help being offered, we can surmise from the context that the motivation was love. A lyric poet from Smyrna, Mimnermus was known for his poems about youth, pleasure and sunlight. We could imagine that the story of Medea was given as an example of the power of love to overwhelm the young.

Direct testimony from the early archaic period only gives tantalising glimpses of Medea, but references in later works indicate that there was a much stronger tradition than we might think. In Pausanias' *Description of Greece*, written c. AD 150, he gives us snippets of information about Medea gathered from a number of different sources, such as Hellanios and Kinaithon. In particular, he includes details of a poem called *Korinthiaka*, by the poet Eumelos, who was writing c. 730 BC. Pausanias tells us that in this poem the Korinthians summoned Medea to Korinth and declared her their queen. This accords with a tradition recorded in a fragment of the poet Simonides, who also says that Medea was queen in Korinth (West (1971), fr. 545 referring to Jason, 'He settled in Korinth, he did not dwell / in Magnesia; and living with his Kolchian wife / he ruled over Thranos and Lechaeum'). Pausanias also records that Eumelos included a version of the story in which Medea's children died by accident as she tried to make them immortal. This story can be supplemented by a further reference to Eumelos found in the scholia to Pindar, *Olympian* (13. 74 g), which says that Medea averted a famine in Korinth by sacrificing to Demeter and the Lemnian nymphs. Later Zeus fell in love with Medea, but she refused his advances out of respect for Hera. As a mark of her gratitude, Hera offered to make Medea's children immortal, and when they died the Korinthians honoured them with a cult.

Clearly the *Korinthiaka* contained a great deal of interesting material, but it is difficult to assess the importance of this text from the handful of references that remain. Pausanias was collecting this information many centuries after the supposed composition of the poem. We do not know whether he obtained his information first hand from the poem (unlikely), or second hand via digests or a mythological tradition which had converted a written story back into oral folklore. It is also problematic that Pausanias was interested in local details, often linked to specific sites or objects of interest. The Korinthian stories he tells may have been confined to that specific locale and linked to particular developments. As we lack a clear context for these snippets of the *Korinthiaka* we may be tempted to generalise to a more pan-Hellenic tradition, and to overestimate the significance of these details. We know little of Eumelos or the purpose for which he wrote his poem, and while he may have simply recorded the traditions of local mythology, he may have been shaping and/or altering them for his own immediate purposes. As a source, Eumelos' *Korinthiaka* via

Pausanias is frustratingly difficult to use, and similar problems confront us when we read Pausanias' comments about another ancient epic, *Naupaktia*, in which it is said that Jason and Medea went to Kerkyra (*Naupaktia* fr. 9. *PEG* – 2.3.9).

These are the sorts of issues which arise when dealing with sources from the archaic period which are only reported, summarised or quoted by later sources. The poets Pherekydes, Simonides and Ibykos are all said by later sources to have written about Medea, but we no longer have direct access to them. What we can say with relative certainty is that even at an early stage, there were several different strands to the story in circulation, and we will see in the next chapter how this has a bearing on questions about the origins of the story.

SOURCES: PINDAR

Pindar was born in Boeotia around 518 BC, and travelled all over the Greek world consorting with the most powerful people of his day, such as the Sicilian tyrant Hieron. Every Pindaric poem takes as its starting point a victory in one of the many sporting competitions open to the aristocracy of Greece. Although we do not know exactly how the poems were composed, they were commissioned by the victor or his family, and Pindar was paid for his work. These circumstances of production meant that the poet would inevitably look to present the victor in the most positive light, and mythology was often made to serve this end. Mythological stories which cast the victor's ancestors in a positive light were popular, as were stories that illustrated the virtues which the victor had shown. Although composed for specific occasions, Pindar's poetry shows wider interests in themes of divine favour, the importance of hard work, or the value of song. The mythology of these poems is designed to support the overall point of the poem. However, Pindar's use of mythology is not a crude distortion of the stories to fit a commercial purpose. His allusions to myth are erudite and often elliptical, assuming that the audience is familiar with the background story and mentioning only certain details. While Pindar certainly did innovate in his treatment of mythology, and shaped it to his own concerns, he was not randomly making things up. Because each poem is tailored to the precise situation in hand, his reading of the myth is not consistent, giving two very different pictures of Medea. *Pythian* 4 presents her as a victim of Aphrodite's love charm, whereas in *Olympian* 13.53–54 she seems more in control, and is referred to as 'Medea who put her love before her father / to save the Argo and its crew' (translated Nisetich 1980).

SOURCES: FIFTH-CENTURY TRAGEDY

Speaking generally, it is because of the desire of the tragic poets for the marvellous that so varied and inconsistent an account of Medea has been given out.

(Diodorus Siculus, 4. 56)

This quotation indicates the contribution made to the development of the myth by the dramatists of fifth-century Athens, and in Chapter 6 we will focus on the surviving play telling the story, Euripides' *Medea* produced in 431 BC. In that chapter we will look at the range of other plays which featured different elements in Medea's life, such as the rejuvenation of Aison. At this point we should note some key features of tragedy which are central to our understanding of myth. The tragedies of fifth-century Athens were produced for Athens, funded as a civic venture by the city, and were staged in competition, encouraging the playwrights to cater to the interests of an Athenian audience. The plays are often Athenocentric, glorifying Athens and giving the city a central role in stories which have their geographical basis elsewhere. For example, the *Oresteia* of Aeschylus begins in Argos but ends with the resolution of the cycle of revenge in an Athenian court, and Euripides' *Herakles* takes place in Thebes but ends with Theseus' offer of a home in Athens. We will see in Chapter 6 that in Euripides' play the arrival of Athenian king Aigeus is more than a convenient plot device, and makes Athens central to the action of the play. Tragedy was highly influential over the development of Medea's myth, but we should be careful to note the precise circumstances in which it was written. The tendency of Attic playwrights to produce a detailed focus on one moment in a story allowed for the greater exploration of motivation and the underlying patterns of a myth, features which are useful for us when constructing a narrative. However, the importance of winning the competition encouraged innovation, and may have taken the myth away from its earlier or strongest associations.

Beyond the plays which survive or are referred to by others, there are two other associated sources which provide information about the myth. First, the *scholia*, critical notes written in later periods and attached to plays. The scholia to Euripides' *Medea* line 264 refer to another tradition that the Korinthians killed the children because they didn't like being ruled by a foreign woman. The scholia to *Medea* line 9 report that the Korinthians were said to have paid Euripides five talents to produce this version of the story, a considerable sum as five talents in the mid fifth century was approximately thirty years' wages for a labourer. The intention was to shift the blame for the death of the children from their ancestors to Medea. Whether or not there is any truth in this story, it raises a significant point, that playwrights could deliberately change myths for a number of different purposes.

Secondly there is the *hypothesis* to a play, a short introduction added at a later date which gives some background information. The hypothesis to Euripides' *Medea* says that Aristotle and Dikaiarchos believed that Euripides derived his drama from a similar one by Neophron. Thus, despite the Athenocentricity of the genre, tragedy throws up a great deal of information about a mythological tradition beyond the limits of the plays which have survived.

SOURCES: THE HELLENISTIC PERIOD

In Chapter 7 we will look at the ways in which the myth travelled from the Greek to the Roman world via the cultures of the Hellenistic period. Our main source from Hellenistic Greece is the epic poem, *Argonautica* of Apollonios Rhodios. Writing in the third century BC, Apollonios was a scholar as much as a poet, producing work which was detailed and intertextual. Although his Medea is the young princess who meets Jason for the first time, there are constant reminders of her future which create an ominous mood. The Hellenistic poets were highly self-conscious and wrote for an educated audience. They were often literary critics and antiquarians with interests in ritual aetiologies, long-forgotten details and the interplay of different versions of a story. For example, the first surviving literary reference we have to Medea's attempt to kill Theseus comes from the Hellenistic 'epic' poem *Hekale* by Kallimachos, another scholar/poet and keeper of the Alexandrian Library. In this poem the traditional grand concerns of epic were rejected in favour of the small-scale encounter between the hero and an old woman which becomes the centre of narrative attention. This desire to focus on arcane knowledge is useful for us today as it has saved a great deal of material which might otherwise have been lost. On the other hand, there was a trend in this period to indulge in recondite detail and to portray extravagant sentiment in extreme baroque fashion, both in literature and art.

The desire to appear learned and to express a particular artistic ideal created a peculiar form of mythological presentation, but Medea's role adapted to changing global priorities. The Hellenistic period witnessed a shift away from the community-based identities of previous generations. Instead of an individual defining his identity via his polis or country, the cosmopolitan ethos of Alexandria encouraged the formation of self-image via other routes. In such a political climate, some of the old Greek issues about race and 'otherness' manifested themselves in different ways. For some, religious or class affinity became the prime factor in determining identity, so that the barbarian 'otherness' of Medea may have been less of an issue. However, it is clear that ethnic identity was still an important feature of many people's lives, as indicated in Theocritus' *Idyll* 15, where a joke is made about Greeks speaking in different dialects. Even though the new society of Alexandria encouraged integration, there was still a tendency to define character negatively by creating a figure of 'the other'.

SOURCES: ROMAN INTERPRETATIONS

When we move to the Roman world we find that Medea was a source of interest from an early stage. There were versions of her story told by the earliest great writers, such as Ennius, and she continued to excite the imagination of later writers. Ovid (c. 43 BC–AD 17) returns to her story in several places in his poetry, most memorably writing a letter from Medea to Jason (*Heroides* 12) and giving an account of her life story in *Metamorphoses* Book 7. He is also said to have composed a tragedy about her life which was praised as a great work of art by his contemporaries. Ovid seems to have been drawn to Medea because of the very complexity of her nature. He was interested in the different aspects of her character, her powers of transformation, and her ambiguous role in male/female relationships.

By contrast, Seneca created a black-hearted witch, and used her story to indulge in gruesome descriptions of madness and magic. Seneca was tutor to the young Nero and became his political adviser when Nero became emperor in AD 54. Close to the highest circles of power in Roman life, and party to all its attendant intrigues and dangers, he was eventually forced to commit suicide in AD 65 after a plot to assassinate the emperor. In addition to his political interests, Seneca was a Stoic philosopher, interested in ideas of controlling passion through rationality. He wrote versions of many myths which had previously been treated by the Greek playwrights. His plays show the influence of his political and philosophical interests, but may also be read as a response to the changing tastes of the Roman public, which were increasingly bloodthirsty. His Medea is very different from Euripides' character.

The most interesting fact about Medea's role in Rome is that she was very popular. In Chapter 7 we will consider the reasons for this popularity, but we should note that Ovid at least was exploring the myth and responding to it in ways that we might find congenial to our own enquiry today.

SOURCES: LITERARY COMPENDIA

The *Bibliotheca* or *Library of Mythology* by Apollodoros is a compendium of mythological stories aimed at producing a systematic and comprehensive account of Greek myth, indicating different variants and the shared characters. The date and authorship of this work is disputed, but it is possible that the author was Apollodoros of Athens, a scholar working in Alexandria in the second century BC who was known to have written about the Greek gods. As the *Bibliotheca* focuses mainly on heroic mythology it is possible that it was a companion to another work, *On the Gods*, which detailed mythology concerning divinities. A similar problem of dating is found with Hyginus' *Fabulae*, a collection of short summaries of stories which is generally thought to have been produced between the first century BC and the first century AD.

The writer Diodorus Siculus (first century BC) produced a *Library*, which aimed at recounting history down to 60 BC. Only 15 of the 40 books survive, including much of the early material such as geographical and mythological surveys. Diodorus drew on a number of earlier sources, and made some critical judgements about their value (including the view of the tragic poets' treatment of Medea, quoted above). His work has a tendency to downplay supernatural features of the stories: for example, he makes Hekate a historical queen who discovers the use of herbal drugs.

By contrast, the late fourth-century AD Orphic *Argonautica* plays up the supernatural aspects of the tale, but reduces Medea's role in the capture of the Golden Fleece, and gives the majority of magical powers to Orpheus, who narrates the story. This transference of mythical story further indicates the malleability of myth.

SOURCES: VISUAL ART

We have predominantly focused on literary accounts which can be explicit in their reading of the motivations and mythological significances of the story. We should not, however, ignore the visual arts of the ancient world. In a society where literacy was limited, visual storytelling could be as important as the verbal. While at times we can see how visual art, such as vase painting, could be a response to a literary form, the traditions are often closer to the fluid material of oral narrative which we noted at the start of this chapter, and can indicate different ways of telling the story. Interpreting visual images requires different skills and approaches to those we use when handling literary texts. The illustrations in this volume, therefore, are limited to allow discussion of each image rather than providing lots of pictures which appear to reinforce the written narrative.

As Carpenter (1991) explains:

> The depiction of myth in the visual arts uses a 'language' quite different from literary languages . . . the relation between the form and the subject also has an effect on the language – the focus of the sculptor preparing a pedimental group of the battle of the gods and giants for a public building such as a temple is obviously different in many ways from that of a vase-painter putting the same subject on the inside of a drinking cup to be sold to a private individual. (pp. 8–9)

We must ask how an image would be viewed, and how the figure of Medea could be seen to relate to that immediate context. For example, was a vase predominantly to be used by men or women? Was it a burial offering, or used for mixing wine at a party? What was the difference for the Romans in seeing Medea depicted on the walls of their home or on a sarcophagus? The earliest images we have of Medea come from around 630 BC and centre on her killing of Pelias/rejuvenating a ram in a cauldron. These images can be paralleled with early Italian scenes suggesting a process of artistic interaction accompanied the development of trade; see Smith (1999). Scenes of rejuvenation continue to be popular into the fifth century, and emphasise a side of Medea's powers which the literary sources can tend to elide.

Figure 1 shows a scene from a red-figure hydria produced in Athens c. 485–470 BC, a vase used primarily for transporting and storing water, and thus associated more with women. The two figures are named 'Medeia' and 'Jason'. Medea, on the left, is shown scattering herbs from a bowl in her left hand. In the centre, a large cauldron is placed on a tripod over a blazing fire, and a ram is leaping out towards Medea. The figure on the right is named as 'Jason' and is shown as an elderly man, with white hair and a staff. It has been suggested that the inscription is mistaken, and should refer to Aison, Jason's father. However, it may be that the artist did intend to show Jason's rejuvenation, and that attempts to condemn the artist for a mistake only betray our overreliance on literary sources. The scene has been composed with considerable care, from the dynamic poses of the humans and the ram, to the details of the ram's horns or Medea's earring. The attitude of the characters is difficult to judge, but Jason's outstretched arm may imply a request that Medea should rejuvenate him as the ram has been returned to its former vigour.

Figure 1 Red-figure hydria showing Medea, Jason and the rejuvenation of a ram. Attic, c. 430 BC.

This is not a scene we have in early literary sources, and this difference of emphasis already alerts us to one of the discrepancies we may encounter when accessing mythology via written and visual sources. Although there is often considerable overlap, the traditions of literary and plastic art have their own interests and motifs. The Golden Fleece most famously is shown in art with Jason being disgorged by the dragon, Athena looking on, with no role for Medea. Just as with literary representations, the context for images can affect the interpretation, as images for one community or one person contain different messages about the story.

We will see in Chapter 7 that after Euripides' *Medea* of 431 BC, there is a shift to representations of Medea in oriental dress, and to scenes showing the dragon chariot and the death of the children at her hands. There are also images which give us views of stories which are not referred to in the written art at this period, as with the red-figure pots from around 450 BC which show Theseus and a woman, presumed to be Medea – this story is not well-attested in the literary sources. Similarly the death of Talos at Medea's hands receives its first literary account in Apollonios' *Argonautica*, but is seen earlier in vases from the last quarter of the fifth century. There are several good sources for the extant artistic images, detailed in the Guide to Further Reading. There are also some literary references to artistic sources, such as Pausanias' comments on physical objects, or such as Pliny's reference to a painting of Medea by Timarchus in the mid first century BC (Pliny, *Natural History* 35.136), discussed by Gutzwiller (2004).

OVERVIEW

Each of the sources mentioned above gives us information about the myth of Medea, from coherent narratives to snapshots and fragmentary hints of a story. No one source can encompass the full range of meanings, as each was composed for a particular audience and a particular occasion. Although a chronological account of the development of the myth contains useful information about the relative merits of each instantiation, it is not enough in itself to give us the keys to understand such a complex figure. Such an approach, often termed diachronic, may elide or obscure connections by insisting on a strict idea of temporal progression. In the next chapter we will therefore treat this material synoptically, that is to say, casting an eye over the whole spectrum, looking for themes and recurrent motifs within all the versions, which will indicate some of the central issues which relate to Medea.

KEY THEMES

3

ORIGINS, FOLKTALE
AND STRUCTURALISM

This chapter will focus on some of the central issues in the study of
mythology in the modern western world. All three sections present
ways to place Medea in context, to find a framework to help us understand such a complex figure. We begin with the question of origins,
then move to a discussion of the terminology categorising some stories
as 'mythology' and others as 'folktale'. We will see that the myth of
Medea contains several elements which can be paralleled in stories
from other cultures. A crosscultural approach to myth is often linked
to the theoretical approach of structuralism, the final topic of this
chapter. While all of these discussions involve ways to divide up the
material and attempts to find coherent structures, they also offer
explanations for the power and longevity of the myth, and so form an
important backdrop to later chapters.

ORIGINS

In the beginning was . . .

And there we run into trouble. Although the origins of myth
command our attention we have nothing secure on which to base
our theories about the origins of Medea's story, or indeed most of
the stories of Greek myth. This lack of evidence has not stopped
generations of theorists from proposing a range of ideas about myth,
story and religion, giving different weight to historical, archaeological
or ideological data. The ideas contained within this section have not

been developed independently about Medea, but represent a number of schools of thought about the wider issues of Greek myth, its formation and its place within the Greek world.

By the time Medea makes an appearance in art or literature she already has a well-formed body of material around her, linked to the story of Jason and the Argonauts. As noted in the previous chapter, our first references to her come in the seventh-century epic *Nostoi*, and in Hesiod's *Theogony*, referring to her marriage to Jason, and vases from the same period indicate the story of the death of Pelias. Given the wide range of episodes, and the geographical distance which these stories encompass, some critics, such as Lesky (1931, 48–50), have argued that there were originally two figures called Medea, whose stories became conflated. The one Medea is believed to be an early figure from Korinthian mythology, and is linked to the stories of the death of her children in that community. The other is believed to be a figure associated with the Kolchian sun-god lineage, through her father, Aietes, and aunt Kirke. Ancient mythographers tried different ways of linking Medea's stories together, such as the argument of Eumelos (cited by Pausanias, 2.1.1 ff.) that made the descendants of Helios the original rulers of Korinth. It is impossible to say which elements were originally part of the myth, whether one 'Medea' came before another. Many scholars think it unlikely that two figures with the same unusual name should coexist, and the 'Unitarian Theory', that there was only ever one figure of Medea, is presented persuasively by Giannini (2000). As Medea arrives in our earliest references with a well-developed mythological persona it is impossible to say where the trail began.

If we cannot find a fixed starting point, we may be able to define the area of Medea's mythic conception. In his 1994 analysis of the myth of Jason and Medea, Moreau argues that Medea was originally a goddess in the tradition of an earth mother, and became an individual figure at a later period, a process termed 'hypostasis'. Moreau's reading stems from a view of Greek religion which looks for core sets of ideas and beliefs, arguing that several individual figures of mythology can develop from one initial figure, such as the 'earth mother'. Johnston (1997) has argued on a related line that Medea was originally a goddess comparable to Hera, but as divine functions became specialised and divided, Medea became a separate figure (see further Chapter 4). As a character, Medea's origins are always divine, as she is part of the family of Helios. The idea that her mythic identity developed from a religious status as a goddess is attractive because the figure of Hekate, to whom Medea is strongly linked, also undergoes a process of mythological reassignment. A child of the Titans, she is accepted into the Olympian pantheon, and her functions change. In Hesiod's *Theogony* (vv. 404–52) Zeus welcomes Hekate, and she takes on a number of roles, from care of the young to overseeing horsemanship. She is linked to Artemis and Demeter in Greek mythology, and until the fifth century she is usually represented as a young woman, similar to Artemis, but carrying torches rather than a bow. It is only in later art that she is depicted more as the old woman, or 'crone'. Some have suggested that Hekate was originally a mother goddess or earth goddess, and her function as a patron of the magical arts is a later development. Such parallels are suggestive for the interpretation of Medea, but it is significant that Hekate is always a goddess, whereas Medea's status as heroine is more problematic.

Readings such as those of Moreau or Johnston are dismissed by some scholars as being 'reductionist', a term referring to attempts to trace all related figures back to single sources. Such 'reductionist' approaches, which seek to explain complex phenomena in terms of simpler phenomena ('reducing' complex stories), are thought by many to be fundamentally flawed, because they cannot take adequate account of the multiplicity of detail, and must ignore material or ideas which cannot be easily schematised or catalogued. By contrast, Dowden (1989) and others would emphasise the multivalency of myth, and the need to view heroines of myth in terms of wider significances. We can explore patterns within a myth without insisting on an overall theory which can explain every aspect. An anti-reductionist approach to the story of Medea might accept that there are elements of the myth which have underlying connections with other themes or characters, but still insist that Medea is an individual figure who needs to be analysed in her own terms. As often with the study of mythology, there is no easy resolution to this issue, and the 'true' answer may well lie somewhere between these two positions, so that Medea was both an individualised figure and part of a wider set of ideas about divinity. The western philosophical tradition would reject such a solution on principle, but dualistic thinking is not the only way to approach such issues. Medea may be both/and, rather than either/or.

ACCRETION AND SUBSTITUTION

Even if we decide to accept as a premise that the 'original' Medea was a goddess, we have to take account of the significant contribution made to her myth by the additional elements which attached themselves. It is possible that several strands of the same story developed and wove back into each other, and that stories which originally were told of other figures gradually became associated with the name of Medea through a process of accretion. Such a process certainly operated in the case of Herakles and Theseus, and there is no reason to doubt that the figure of Medea could have exerted a similar pull over stories which shared some thematic links to her core story. This would account for the range of material which forms the 'myth of Medea', but we should remember that the processes of accretion/hypostasis/adaptation were all working before the creation of our earliest extant sources, so any statement about Medea's origins must remain speculative. Some have suggested Medea's myth is complicated because she *supplanted* other earlier figures: Will (1955) suggested that originally it was Kirke who helped Jason capture the Golden Fleece. This may be an idea which Valerius' Flaccus refers to in his *Argonautica*: Venus decides to help Jason by disguising herself as Kirke, then tells Medea that Jason had asked for her help, and advises her to give it. In other versions of the story, Medea goes to Kirke for advice and purification after the murder of Apsyrtos.

One final point worth noting on the issue of origins is the idea that both Jason and Medea have links with healing. There may have been an early narrative pattern about medicine, and in Chapter 4 we will see how healing arts could be associated with magic. Jason was tutored by the famed healer Cheiron, and Mackie (2001) has argued that Jason was originally the one with the powers to heal, and that Medea gradually eclipsed him. Mackie's argument is speculative, but thought provoking. He calls attention to the name 'Jason', which means

'Healer', and suggests that early poets hinted at Jason's medicinal skills, a talent shared by many of Cheiron's pupils. The stories of Jason and Medea may have become intertwined because of this link, but the evidence for Mackie's argument is inevitably elliptical, and thus difficult to pursue.

From all of our discussions so far it is clear that we cannot return to an original figure, and some theorists would say that there is no such thing as an 'original' anyway, as every time a story is told it owes something to past ideas or its immediate surroundings. Medea's origins lie in a murky soup of ideas about divinity, society and identity which we will explore more fully in later chapters. If we cannot find a point of origin from which to construct a linear account, we must look to other ways to order and/or understand the story, and the remaining sections of this chapter will focus on different ways of contextualising and making the story meaningful.

FOLKTALE

So far, we have been discussing the 'myth' of Medea, so to introduce the subheading 'Folktale' implies that we will be discussing a different category of story. Unfortunately, the situation is not as simple as it may seem, for the terms 'myth', 'folktale' and 'legend' do not have precise meanings. They can be defined in a number of ways, so that any particular story may belong to one or more categories, depending on individual judgement. The terms themselves do not provide any real assistance, for the term 'myth', as we noted earlier, comes from the Greek *muthos* meaning 'story'. Similarly, the term 'folk' comes from the Germanic *volk*, meaning 'the people', so a folktale is simply a 'story of the people'. If the terminology is so closely related, where does the distinction come from?

The methodology of analysing folktales originates in the work of the Grimm brothers in the nineteenth century. They compiled a compendium of 'folktales' drawn from stories which had been orally transmitted. They observed that similar stories could be found in many different cultures, and from this a lively intellectual debate was sparked as scholars attempted to explain the recurrence of story patterns.

A number of theories were suggested and developed over the years. Some suggested a process of transmission from one culture to another. At the other extreme, it was suggested that recurrent story patterns were evidence of psychological 'hardwiring', a set of patterns common to human nature which manifested itself in the same set of stories, an approach similar to Jungian theories of archetypes (see Chapter 1). One of the most useful developments to come from this work was the systematic compilation of story-types which could be crossreferenced. The initial work by Aarne was supplemented by Thompson, creating the standard textbook for referring to folktale types: *The Types of the Folktale: A Classification and Bibliography* (Thompson, 1961). Folktales are referred to by their place in this catalogue, so AT or AAT (for 'Aarne-Thompson') 510AB is the tale of Cinderella, and AT313 is the girl who helps the hero.

From this compendium it is obvious that many of the stories we know of as 'Greek myth' can be paralleled in other cultures, and so may with reason be called 'folktales'. Certainly there was a strong oral tradition in Greece, but what we have before us as 'Greek myth' is composed of consciously shaped artistic products, literature or art. This blurs distinctions which emphasise the need for a myth to have a force or purpose which may be lacking in folklore, for if an artist shapes a folktale, does this imbue it with greater meaning and transform it into a myth? Is there any essential difference between the stories we call 'folktales' and those we call 'myth'? Hansen (2002) attempts to distinguish between the categories, with the principle that 'myths' are more serious, related to historical events or issues, and are fixed to a specific place, whereas folktales are 'migratory narratives' which can adapt and move across boundaries of society and period. However, he notes the case of Medea as one where the two overlap. A short volume such as this provides no space for a fuller treatment of the subject, so we will need to content ourselves with a survey of the elements of Medea's story which can most easily be paralleled in what are commonly termed 'folktales'. The purpose of this discussion is to elicit parallels which tell us about the significance of the story of Medea.

THE 'HELPER-MAIDEN'

The most striking parallel is with AT313 'helper-maiden'. In this story pattern, a young girl goes out of her way to assist a hero. She is usually a subsidiary character in the main story of the hero, and often has a happy ending. She can be clever and possess valuable skills, as does the Scandinavian figure of the 'mastermaid'. In Greek myth, the exemplar of this figure is Nausikaa in Homer's *Odyssey* Book 6. When the hero, Odysseus, is shipwrecked on Scheria, he is found by Nausikaa, who provides him with practical assistance and advice which enables him to continue his journey. Although Nausikaa does not marry Odysseus, the narrative explicitly mentions her marriageable status, implying the story pattern. Another famous example is that of Ariadne, who helps Theseus to negotiate the maze when he comes to kill the Minotaur. In that story, Ariadne seems to achieve the traditional reward and is taken away by Theseus. Unfortunately, the story does not have a happy ending, as Theseus abandons Ariadne on Naxos. There is an ironic reference to this variant in Apollonios' *Argonautica* when Jason attempts to persuade Medea to help him (Book 3, 997 ff.). He cites Ariadne as a positive example for Medea to follow, apparently oblivious to the implication that like Theseus he would abandon Medea, his helper-maiden. For the audience of the poem, there is the irony that although the assistance of the maiden ends badly for Ariadne, in this case it is the hero, Jason, who ultimately will come off worse.

Medea clearly falls into the category of helper-maiden in the initial stages of the story of the Golden Fleece, as without her magical skills Jason would be unable to fulfil the tasks set by Aietes. However, the following episodes of Medea's life story move away from this category, making her less a helper-maiden and more a powerful figure in her own right. Accounts of the early stage of the myth often retroject the later characterisation, so that the function of helper-maiden is overshadowed by hints of the later dangerous persona. This is certainly the case in Apollonios' *Argonautica*, where there are frequent ominous references to the later stages of Medea's life, even though her actions in helping Jason are outwardly the acts of a helper-maiden.

The other strong pattern which relates to the first stage of Medea's life history is that of the young woman who leaves her father for love, or betrays her homeland. In discussions of Graeco-Roman mythology this story pattern is sometimes referred to as the Tarpeia pattern, a reference to the story of Tarpeia, who is said to have betrayed Rome to the Sabines (discussed by Bremmer and Horsfall, 1987). Medea can be portrayed in this way, as a victim of love or as a trophy to be won. There are, however, problems caused by the status of the Golden Fleece. The order of events runs counter to the traditional story pattern, whereby a hero must accomplish dangerous tasks in order to win the hand of the princess. As Clauss (1997, 157) observes, 'to conquer Medea is to win the fleece, the opposite of the usual folktale motif which has the young hero perform the contest to win the bride'.

The story of 'Jason and Medea' contains many motifs which suggest further folktale paradigms, such as the Quest story which Radermacher (1943) and others have seen in the tale of the Golden Fleece. The death of the children by Medea's deliberate or accidental design has some links to AT1119, the story of the ogre who kills his own children, and numerous details of magic, the outsider and the ability to fly are seen in other tales across the world. There are undoubtedly a number of parallels which can be drawn, but what do these links to folktale mean for our understanding of the myth?

Hansen (2002) in his preface to a book on folktale argues that 'since such stories tend not to be fixed in form, each text manifests variations in detail that reflect in interesting ways the culture, time and occasion in which it finds itself, the particular narrator/host/audience'. An understanding of folktale can help us to explore the place of a myth in a society, and enables us to see how the myth of Medea diverges significantly from traditional story patterns. Just as Medea herself breaks conventional norms, so the story itself draws attention to the pattern only to disrupt it: the helper-maiden becomes a bane; the princess is the instrument of the hero's success rather than the prize; the girl chooses husband over father, then turns on the husband. An understanding of folktale highlights just how peculiar the figure of Medea really is.

FOLKTALE, MYTH AND OLD WIVES' TALES

The study of folktale can also enhance our appreciation of the myth by providing a differently gendered reading. The literary tradition from which we have received most of our information is male-dominated, through production, performance and transmission. There may have been layers of folktale in Greek culture which were lost, particularly those told by women. In the following chapters we will see that other aspects of Medea's story may be linked to undercurrents about women and children which are not so obvious in the traditions we have received. Recent work on folktale has itself emphasised the ways in which male scholarship has taken over a form of storytelling which was traditionally the province of women, imposing an anti-female bias on the material. The way that Medea may be relegated to a subsidiary role in the schematisation of folktale, as 'helper-maiden', may be due to male bias. Another, more gender-neutral, analysis views Medea as central to her own tale, the focus of attention in herself, rather than as an adjunct to the story of another. We will explore this issue in more detail in Chapter 5.

STRUCTURALISM

Ideas of schematisation lead us to the approach of structuralism. Viewed from this theoretical perspective, the myth of Medea can be understood by paying attention to the relationship of its constitutive elements. Recurrent motifs, such as the murder of kin, the rejuvenation of others, or the repeated act of fleeing from a situation, can be viewed as essential to the creation of meaning. When we are alert to patterns in a myth, we can perceive more parallels, and also note when there are unusual divergences from the expected pattern. This approach treats myth as having an underlying system, so can help us both to understand Medea's story and to place it in the wider context of Greek mythology.

The term 'structuralism' originated in the study of language, and is related to the wider field of 'semiotics', the study of signs. The central principle of this idea was that individual elements (of a language, picture, story, etc.) have no intrinsic meaning, but only become mean-ingful when they are combined with others in a structure (hence, 'structuralism'). A good introduction to the principles of structuralism can be found in Barry (1996, 39–60). From these intellectual principles developed a style of academic study which analysed language, or any other system, purely in formal, objective terms, looking for structures. One of the most powerful structures comes from the idea of binary oppositions, two terms which between them cover the whole range of possibility and mutually define each other, so 'light and dark', 'up and down': light cannot exist without the idea of dark; there is no such thing as up without the opposite, down, and so on. This sort of approach is particularly useful when studying the Greek world, where the idea of thinking in pairs was widespread, such as in the con-struction of ethnic identities: Greek speakers versus 'barbarians' (= non-Greek speakers, literally 'those who say barbarbar'). Again, this is a matter we will return to in Chapter 5.

LÉVI-STRAUSS

The ideas of structuralism were first applied to the realm of mythology by Claude Lévi-Strauss, who brought a scientific approach to the collated parallels of folktale in different cultures. He argued that the folktale patterns are made up of a number of repeated elements which become significant when combined with others, so the symbols of 'sea' or 'eagle' take on a place in the wider context of, for example, 'the wilderness' or 'divine powers'. These individual units he called 'mythemes' (after the term 'phoneme' used in linguistics to describe the smallest unit of sound). Lévi-Strauss' analysis of the myth of Oidipous breaks down the story into individual elements, such as 'Oidipous kills his father', and then compares it with other elements of the story in an almost mathematical model. The story of Medea, then, could be seen to be composed of many different mythemes, such as the capture of the Golden Fleece, the killing of a brother, the various acts and attributes of the magician.

At its most basic level, structuralist analysis goes no further than enumerating the elements and delineating the structure of the myth, and creating a synchronic analysis (i.e. one which gives no weight to historical conditions). Although structuralist analysis can be very useful in articulating the feature of a myth, the method is not unproblematic. The comparison with linguistics is seen by many to be fatally flawed. Whereas we may accept that an individual phoneme such as 'p' makes no sense except in combination with others, it is less obvious that an individual mytheme, such as the symbol of the eagle, is meaningless on its own. Structuralist readings of myth are limited and still controversial, despite their claim to conform to scientific standards of argument and demonstrable evidence.

Lévi-Strauss himself made further contributions to the field as he developed an overview of mythology. In some respects this is a distortion of structuralist ideas, which 'should' insist on the articulation of structures and nothing more, but Lévi-Strauss developed a number of ideas about mythology which deserve some consideration. One of the strongest themes came from his argument that the basic structures of mythology were a response to social tensions and reflected the underlying anxieties of a society. He believed that we could strip away all the problems about context and sources which we discussed in the previous chapter, and discover an underlying core structure which would give us the *true meaning* of the story. So the myth of Medea could be deconstructed (i.e. broken down into its component parts) to illustrate certain themes of social tension, such as the foreigner, the insider/outsider.

A fuller discussion of this approach falls outside the scope of this volume, but we will refer to key elements of it at later points in our discussion. The division of material in the next two chapters owes something to structuralist analysis of myth, but will use these distinctions as starting points from which to explore the material, rather than insisting on rigid boundaries and structures as the key to any 'true meaning'.

OVERVIEW

Work on origins, folktale and structuralism speaks of a desire to categorise and provide a quasi-scientific approach to myth. One of the definitions of 'myth' which is sometimes offered is that it provides an 'ordering of experience', it gives us patterns and ways to think about and communicate issues which are too complicated for the human mind to approach directly. In this respect, the approaches explored in this chapter continue to try to impose order on myth, which is itself already an ordering process. Lévi-Strauss even suggested that structuralist readings of myth were in fact just another variant of the myth under discussion; that is to say, that scholarly analyses are not outside, objective observers of myth, but are part of the same whole.

We have seen that the myth of Medea has many layers and can support different interpretations. While the search for origins is ultimately unsatisfactory, it does indicate that Medea was central to the earliest stages of Greek mythological thinking. The parallels with folktale across different cultures further suggest that her story taps into ideas/fears/beliefs which have recurred throughout human history, and structuralist theory gives us tools to formulate those ideas and examine them in a systematic manner.

This chapter has focused on the processes which compose the myth of Medea. The next two chapters will focus on the substance and content of the myth, seeing it 'in action', engaging with audiences rather than existing as an object under the microscope of critical analysis. One definition of myth is that it is a 'socially significant story', an idea which emphasises the function of a myth. A story must serve some purpose if it is to survive, and when a story has survived for over two and a half millennia we should expect to find something extremely useful or powerful at its heart. In the following chapter we will look at aspects of Medea's story which may be seen as particularly useful in articulating ideas about individual identity. Chapter 5 will then examine ideas which are more relevant to the place of the individual within the wider community.

4

WITCHCRAFT, CHILDREN AND DIVINITY

In this chapter we will focus on three recurrent features of Medea's story across the centuries. All three sections will explore the ways in which we as individuals relate to the big issues, Life and Death. Medea's status on the borders between humanity and divinity makes her a potent symbol for the complexities of mortal life. Even though she has powers usually associated with the gods, she is intimately involved in human struggles: romantic relationships, love of children, loyalty and betrayal. Myth may have a psychological function, as stories are used to articulate ideas which an individual might not be able to face if presented directly. As the individual in the ancient world was largely defined by his or her place within a society, there is an obvious overlap between the psychological and the social functions of myth. This chapter forms a pair with the following chapter, where we will examine themes relating to the social functions of myth.

WITCHCRAFT

The strongest image of Medea in the ancient world was undoubtedly that of the witch, the sorceress using herbs, incantations and innate magical powers to achieve her aims. We saw in Chapter 2 that the earliest sources, literary and artistic, show her as a dangerous magical figure. Her powers are not trivial – she can control natural forces, and even reverse the order of life and death by rejuvenating the old. In this section we will explore the various ways in which Medea can be related to the idea of magic in the ancient world. As a practitioner, she has access to a number of different traditions and techniques of magic, but she can also be presented as a victim of magic, particularly in the area of love magic, an example of the problematic status which characterises much of her mythology.

The figure of the witch can be traced to different folktale elements, but the term 'witch' is problematic. There is no single Greek word meaning 'witch', and the term has acquired a wide range of associations in English which would not necessarily be applicable in the Greek context. This part of the discussion, therefore, will first examine the Greek context of magic and witchcraft, then proceed to a wider discussion of the term 'witch' and its associations in mythological tradition.

DRUGS AND SONG

Magic and witchcraft at a basic level imply abilities or activities outside the realm of normal human existence, things which are 'supernatural', in the literal sense of 'beyond nature'. In the Greek world magic could be attributed both to intrinsic superhuman abilities and to knowledge of special tools. While some figures had innate ability, because of a link to divinity, others were understood to have access to magic via knowledge. Individuals, both in mythology and in real life, could be said to be using 'magic' when they used their knowledge of herbs to achieve various effects. The term *pharmakis* (female), or *pharmakeus/pharmakos* (male), is often used in this context; it is no coincidence that the term gives us the medical 'pharmaceutical', for in a pre-scientific age knowledge of medicine could often be seen as supernatural (see Lloyd, 1979).

In Greek mythology there are many examples of figures who used magical herbs for different purposes. In the *Odyssey* Helen uses magic to soothe her guests (Book 4), while Kirke uses magic to transform men into animals (Book 10), and Hermes shows Odysseus how to use the magic Moly plant for protection. Kirke and Helen had links to the divine, but other people who used magic in ancient literature used more prosaic methods, relying on the magic of the plants, rather than the essential nature of the practitioner. Such practices were often associated with women, particularly in the area of love charms. In tragedy, Deianeira, the wife of Herakles, killed him by using an ill-chosen love potion (the story told in Sophocles' *Trachiniae*); the nurse in Euripides' *Hippolyous* speaks of using a love charm to help Phaidra; and in Euripides' *Andromache*, Hermione accuses Andromache of making her barren by using herbal charms against her (vv. 29–35, 155–60). The use of magic for erotic purposes is also seen in *Idyll* 2 by the Hellenistic poet Theocritos, who shows Simaithea attempting to win back her lover. Medea herself can be seen as a victim of love charms, as in Pindar *Pythian* 4. 214 ff. when Aphrodite deliberately sets out to help Jason. In Apollonios' *Argonautica*, Medea is subjected to a violent attack by Eros, as we will discuss further in Chapter 7.

This idea of the witch is not confined to mythology, for there were legal cases which centred around accusations of witchcraft, as in the case of Demosthenes 25, *Against Aristogeiton* 79–80 (c. 330 BC) which alleges that Theoris was a witch (*pharmakis*) who killed her family with drugs. This case indicates how there are several areas of overlap between sociohistorical issues and literary *topoi.*

Medea has the attributes of a *pharmakis*, as her ability with drugs is central to her magical abilities. The collection of magical herbs is the central idea behind Sophocles' *Rhizotomoi*, and in Ovid's account of her involvement in the death of Pelias (*Metamorphoses* Book 7), it is the crucial omission of the magical herbs from the cauldron which causes the rejuvenation to fail. In the Greek tradition, this associates her strongly with the erotic use of magic, and with eastern traditions, for such abilities were generally believed to be strongest in Asiatic lands.

The use of herbs was not the only aspect of magic which could be accessed by mortals, for the use of spells was also important – in the case of Deianeira and Simaithea, there is an important series of rituals to be performed to ensure the efficacy of the drug. Language was seen as a powerful magical tool in both mythological and real-life situations. In mythology, we think of the power of Orpheus, who was able to charm the rocks with his song, or the Sirens who lured sailors to their death. There are also many historical examples of how words were believed to have power, as individuals wrote spells or created objects with words on them to achieve magical ends. We have surviving examples of papyri and amulets, and many examples of curse tablets, particularly binding curses, called in Greek *katadesmoi* or in Latin *defixiones*. In this context, the power of Medea's voice is important, in that she has the ability to deceive, tricking those around her, be they her own family or the daughters of Pelias.

DIVINE MAGIC

If magical knowledge can be accessed by mortals, Medea also exhibits magical behaviours which are more in keeping with her divine ancestry, and which testify to an innate supernatural ability. She is said to have control over the forces of nature, ability to control the weather and animals, and the ability to fly (albeit with the aid of a chariot). In Corneille's seventeenth-century tragedy Medea has a magic wand and a magic ring, attributes which link her with figures of Faerie. A particular feature of Medea's myth is the ability to inflict psychological harm, a complement to her power to deceive with language. The most powerful demonstration of this ability comes from Apollonios' description of how she causes the death of Talos by casting the evil eye and causing him to fall (*Argonautica* 4. 638–88). The terror of this power is such that it causes the writer to express his shock:

> Then in her incantation she sought to win over the magic help of the Keres, devourers of the spirit, swift dogs of Hades which prowl through all the sky and are set upon mortal men. Three times did she beseech and call upon them with incantations, and three times with prayers. Her mind set on evil, she cast a spell upon bronze Talos' eyes with her malevolent glances; against him her teeth ground out bitter fury, and she sent out dark phantoms in the vehemence of her wrath.
>
> Father Zeus, my mind is all aflutter with amazement, if it is true that death comes to us not only from disease and wounds, but someone far off can harm us, as that man, bronze though he was, yielded to destruction through the grim power of Medea, mistress of drugs. (*Argonautica* 4. 1655 ff., trans. Hunter, 1993)

An alternative version is given by Apollodorous, who suggests that Medea may have caused Talos' death by the same powers of persuasion she used against Pelias: 'According to some she drove him mad with her drugs, while according to others, she promised to make him immortal and pulled out the nail, causing him to die when all the ichor flowed away' (*Bibliotheca* 1.9.26, trans. Hard, 1997).

REJUVENATION

The power of rejuvenation involves several magical themes. This is a motif from folktale, where magic cauldrons are often associated with rejuvenation. The anthropological mythographer Frazer (1922) linked Medea's rejuvenation of Aison with African practices. There are similar stories in western traditions, as in the Welsh story of Llasar Llaes' cauldron told in the fourteenth-century *Mabinogion*. In Graeco-Roman culture rejuvenation can be associated with witches such as Hekate and Erichtho, or with more positive examples as when the deified Herakles rejuvenates Iolaos (as told in Euripides' *Herakleidai*).

However, Medea's rejuvenation is achieved by first killing the subject, then resurrecting him or her as a younger version. This is the ability not simply to rejuvenate, but to bring a figure back to life, which is far more troubling: the great healer Asklepios was himself killed for overstepping cosmic boundaries when he resurrected a man. In Ovid's *Metamorphoses* we get an interesting view of the relative rights and wrongs of such a procedure when Jason asks Medea to transfer some of his life to his father Aison. Medea refuses, saying that such a process is forbidden:

How vile a crime has fallen from your lips!
So I have power to transfer to another
A period of your life! This Hekate
Forbids; not right nor fair is your request.
But more than your request, a greater boon,
I'll aim to give; not with your years I'll dare
The attempt but by my arts, to win again
Your father's years long gone, if but her aid
The three-formed goddess gives and with her presence
Prospers the bold tremendous enterprise.
(*Metamorphoses* 7.166 ff., trans. Melville, 1986)

Medea does rejuvenate Aison after cutting his throat, and her powers so amaze Bacchus that he gets her to perform the same service for his nurses.

The cauldron is generally associated with the dark side of super-natural powers, but it could be seen as having positive associations, as Isler-Kerényi (2000) argues. The symbolism links it both with female regenerative powers, and with ideas of cooking and civilisation, which Halm-Tisserant (1993) and others have analysed. We should note, however, that it is the nature of the herbs which is said to make the difference in Ovid's account, so that the cauldron is not the cause of the magical transformation.

THE MANY FACES OF 'THE WITCH'

A wider analysis of the context of witchcraft returns us to our earlier discussion of folktale, for the figure of the witch is a rich source of ideas in those traditions. Throughout history the figure of the witch has held a tremendous fascination as a point of intersection between two powerful discourses: concern about the divine, and concern about the position of women. In a patriarchal society, this is always likely to be an explosive combination. Recent work on this topic has shown how the figure of the witch has been manipulated in popular and academic circles throughout history. The witch can be constructed as a negative symbol of femininity, the woman with evil intent who provokes fear, as a positive symbol of female power or skill, or as an intrinsically liminal figure pushing the boundaries of different societal categories. All of these approaches can be applied to the story of Medea.

What, then, do we mean today when we describe Medea as a 'witch'? The word brings with it a wide range of associations, often unacknowledged. Is Medea like the Wicked Witch of the West in the *Wizard of Oz*, or the prophetic, manipulative witches of *Macbeth*? Should she be seen in stereotypical terms, with pointy hat and broom-stick? Or is she a victim of male fear of female power or sexuality? Would men today call her not a 'witch', but a 'bitch'?

In many cultures women are particularly associated with nature and, therefore, portrayed as being as wild and unpredictable as the weather. Human fears about the hostile cosmos can be transformed into male fears about women, leading to hatred and negative stereo-typing. Fear of women can be particularly centred around female sexuality, from elaborate procedures to protect virginity to the psychological fear of the *vagina dentata* – a male concern that during intercourse the female will actually bite off his reproductive organs. The story of Medea touches upon many of these fears: a figure who can control the forces of nature, who can rejuvenate as well as give birth, and yet also cuts off a man's line of descendants. In Euripides' version she is also the figure who acts, at least partially, out of wounded sexual pride when she is rejected by Jason. The figure of the witch implies a far more complex set of ideas, values and prejudices than attach to the male equivalents of wizards or warlocks.

CHILDREN

The issue of sexuality and gender which forms part of the nexus of ideas about the witch is related to the fear inspired by Medea's ability to transgress the usual bounds of human behaviour, including love for family. In her escape from Iolkos she is often shown as killing her brother, Apsyrtos, and her own children die as a result of her activities in Korinth. Although there are a number of versions of the death of Medea's children, the most famous version, which perhaps indicates its closeness to the essence of the myth, is the story told by Euripides, that Medea kills her children as an act of revenge for Jason's infidelity. After the production of this play in 431 BC, this becomes a major defining act, but Medea's association with children and the processes of reproduction has more layers to it than this one episode suggests.

Many scholars have focused attention on the status of Medea as a deliberate infanticide, looking at the story in psychoanalytical terms. Such readings may say more about modern concerns than about the ancient view of the myth. Today we may adduce post-partum psychosis as a reason for the killing of newborn infants, or point to more complex reasons for the death of older children whereby the mother experiences a misplaced sense of guilt. Such incidents have been known throughout history (see Hoffer and Hull, 1984). In the UK, there is generally a presumption by the courts that any woman who kills her own children is mentally unstable, but in the US, by contrast, the act is often treated as murder, even when the mother appears to be suffering from post-partum psychosis. The killing of children is generally seen by modern society as one of the greatest evils possible – witness the horror aroused by the Moors Murderers or the murder of child hostages at Beslan in 2004. The myth of Medea may be used by us today to talk about such acts of violence towards children, but does it tell us anything about the myth in its ancient context? In the ancient world, we may see a similar horror expressed by Thucydides when he describes the murder of schoolchildren as the greatest atrocity of the Peloponnesian War (*History of the Peloponnesian War* 7. 29–30). However, this is not a straightforward piece of evidence, as Orwin (1994) has argued that the significance of this story is not the children *per se*, but rather the Athenian politics which caused the situation to develop. While psychoanalytical theories of myth emphasise the universality of human concerns, we should be careful to distinguish between modern and ancient readings, and focus on the context in which the ancient myths are produced. There is, for example, no firm evidence to support Corti's psychoanalytical reading, in which she argues that the myth of Medea is about society's innate hostility towards children.

CHILD KILLING AND SOCIETY

If the psychoanalytical approach runs the risk of anachronism, the Greek and Roman worlds had another manifestation of child killing which the myth of Medea could reflect – infant exposure. There is still much scholarly debate about this ancient practice, whereby unwanted infants were abandoned, thus sparing the parents the blood guilt of directly killing the child. It is difficult to assess the frequency of this practice, and the likelihood of girls rather than boys being exposed. It is also true that many individuals in the ancient world suffered from infertility, so that an exposed child might well be found and adopted by another family.

Nevertheless, the idea of exposing a baby is found in several myths, which may indicate a societal anxiety about this issue. The Trojan War could have been averted if the infant Paris (Alexandros) had been killed, but his mother chose to abandon him instead, and he survived, returning to Troy and eventually destroying the city; Oidipous was exposed by his father to prevent the fulfilment of an oracle, but survived and did as prophesied kill his father and marry his mother; on a happier note, Ion was exposed by his mother after she was raped by Apollo, and is only reunited with her when he is an adult. Although this story pattern has a direct point of reference in the ancient practice of exposure, we should also note the folktale pattern, most commonly known in the western world as the story of 'Babes in the Wood'. The pattern can be linked to a psychological reading, as the child's fear of abandonment. We should note, however, that in sociohistorical times, the decision as to whether a child would be accepted or rejected lay with the father, not the mother, so that the role of Medea is more difficult to parallel.

SOCIAL STRUCTURES AND REPRODUCTION

There is a stronger association with other anxieties about reproduction in the ancient world. It was very important that a man should have a son to continue his family line, someone who would care for family traditions and inherit wealth. In many Greek communities, the role of marriage was to lend a woman to another family in order that a child might be produced *for the man*: in Euripides' play Jason specifically bemoans this necessity (*Medea* vv. 574 ff.), wishing that children could be produced by some new means, which would do away with the need for women entirely. If women could not always be trusted, a man could not always know that the child was truly his, and so women held an important but suspect role in the continuation of the line.

Medea completely reverses this process, destroying Jason's line so that his family will die out. Similarly, by killing her brother Apsyrtos she destroys her own father's family line, in terms of male heirs. She is seen to have the opposite power in Euripides' story, where she is the one who can interpret the oracle and cure Aigeus' sterility. In one sense, Medea has supernatural control over life and death, through her magical skills of rejuvenation etc., but from a simpler perspective she represents the ultimate female power of creating life, something which men have traditionally feared and sought to control.

MEDEA AND HERAKLES

The pattern of killing one's children and yet having control over the forces of life and death can be paralleled in the story of Herakles. The hero who captures Kerberos, the guard dog of hell, and is eventually deified with the power to rejuvenate others, also kills his children. The story, dramatised by Euripides in his *Herakles*, tells how Hera drives Herakles mad, and causes him to kill his three sons. The parallelism between the two figures is suggested by an ancient vase which shows both Medea and Herakles (Figure 2). This red-figure volute krater would have been used for mixing wine and water, and was produced in Apulia (southern Italy) c. 340 BC. It shows Medea and the Paidagogos (children's tutor) inside a temple, with two children seated at the altar, a tableau which seems to reflect the story told by Euripides. To the right of the altar are Herakles and Iris, a possible reflection of the Euripidean play *Herakles*, in which Iris appears as Hera's messenger. To the left of the scene are Nike (Victory), Athena and two youths, and to the right are Demeter and Kore. These last two figures indicate the overall significance of the vase, as a reference to the Eleusinian mysteries – the vase is inscribed 'Temple at Eleusis'. Although Medea herself is not usually associated with this set of cult rituals, the Eleusinian mysteries are associated with Herakles. As a powerful set of stories about life and death, they may plausibly have been associated with Medea in the popular imagination. The vase may also refer to a link made in a version of the story told by Diodorus Siculus (4. 55), where it is Medea who cures Herakles of his madness. We may extrapolate from this that both figures are related to an idea that children are the correct route to immortality, and that those who meddle with the processes of life and death do so at the risk of losing their natural access to immortality via children.

Figure 2 Line drawing of vase showing Medea and Herakles at Eleusis.

CHILD-KILLING DEMONS

There have been a number of analyses of Medea's role which emphasise different aspects of her association with children. Johnston (1995,
1997) has argued that the story should be understood in the context of
wider traditions about dangers to children, and that Medea represents

both sides of the tradition – a figure who initially was seen as a protectress of children, and then as a threat to them.

Infant mortality was high in ancient societies, so this was an appropriate focus of worship. Greek traditions involved a number of figures who were used to talk about threats to children, such as the bogeyman creatures Mormo, Gello or Lamia. In other mythological traditions there are far more stories involving children than we see in the Graeco-Roman mythology. In Celtic and Nordic traditions there are stories of the spirits of unborn children haunting their mothers, and there are traditions about baby-snatching demons in Mesopotamian myths. In Greek mythology, such disturbing trends are generally absent, but there may be a deeper level of storytelling not represented in the literary artistic traditions. Such a background may be relevant to the dream of Klytaimestra (Aeschylus, *Choephori* vv. 523 ff.), in which she gives birth to a snake which then bites her.

The association with the death of children has been questioned by a number of scholars, and we should note that Medea kills the children not because they are hers, but because they are Jason's. She is able to label the children as 'Jason's', and thus the children she kills are at that moment not viewed as 'hers' but 'something of her enemy'. It is also possible that Medea's brother/half-brother Apsyrtos should not be seen as a child, for he is supposed to be an older figure in many accounts of the myth.

DIVINITY AND RITUAL

The first problem to confront us in trying to schematise Medea's relation to gods and men is the question of whether she is mortal or divine. Her mortality is emphasised by Euripides, or rather by the character of Medea in that play (see further Chapter 6). She is also said to have a tomb at Thesprotion, according to Gnaeus Gellius, a second-century BC Roman historian and antiquarian (fr. 9). However, Hesiod in his *Theogony* places her in a list of marriages between gods and mortals suggesting that she is predominantly divine. She is also said in some traditions to be married to Achilles in the Elysian fields, as Hera prophesies in Apollonios Rhodios' *Argonautica* (4. 810–15).

Medea is, perhaps, best described as a heroine, though that term is not itself easy to define. The term 'hero' encompasses a range of possible statuses in the Greek world, predominantly referring to figures who are between mortal and divine, often because of divine parentage, or who transcend the divide on their death and subsequently become an object of cult worship. There is a further problem in that the feminine form 'heroine' does not seem to have been a common Greek usage. Fortunately, there have been a number of scholarly accounts which attempt to address this problem, notably Lyons (1997). Her conclusion makes the following judgement about the status of heroes and heroines:

> mortals and immortals need one another for self-definition, and heroines and heroes, as the intermediate category, are necessary to both because they allow a working out of the tensions and ambiguities inherent in a system of anthropomorphic divinities worshipped by a society that glorified the works of human beings. The Greeks knew how much their gods depended on them and told their myths to prove it. (Lyons, 1997, 127)

MEDEA AND THE GODS

From the earliest period Medea is associated with a number of gods. She is the granddaughter of Helios, the sun god, and is linked to Hera and Aphrodite in Korinth (Plutarch, *De Herod. malig.* 871b). The link to Aphrodite is part of the story of her relationship with Jason, but the link to Hera goes far deeper. Hera's sphere of influence, including marriage and childbirth, covers many of the same areas as does Medea's. We noted above that some have argued that Medea herself was originally part of Hera's manifestations. Medea is also linked to early concepts of divinity expressed as the figures of Demeter/Hekate as mother or earth goddess, and the role of Hekate as moon goddess further links Medea to Artemis. In some variants Aietes receives an oracle which tells him that he will be killed by a foreigner, and he appoints Medea as priestess of Artemis with the task of killing foreigners, a motif we will return to in the next chapter.

There is no single pattern for Medea's place in the divine sphere, and artistic sources in the classical period do not stress her associations with the Olympian gods. The main narratives make Medea a powerful force in her own right. Indeed, Kovacs (1993) has shown how there is a striking lack of divine participation in Euripides' play, and Medea herself claims to be acting as an agent of Zeus' justice. As a figure who is never punished for acts which would normally be seen as criminal and/or sacrilegious, Medea seems to exist outside the boundaries of classical Greek religion.

MEDEA AND HEKATE

Medea is, however, strongly linked to the figure of Hekate, a goddess who herself occupies an ambiguous position in Greek religion. Hekate appears to have originally been a multifaceted goddess whose darker, negative attributes were given greatest prominence. In the earliest literary reference, Hesiod's *Theogony* 404–52, she is praised for her gifts, and called a protectress of the young. Other features associate her with weddings, horsemanship and competitions.

Johnston (1999, 205–11) argues that Hekate was originally a goddess in Caria, where she guarded cities, and her sphere of influence became doorways and transitions, extending to a wider cosmic role. Other scholars have linked Hekate to early figures of a mother goddess, or an earth goddess. In classical and later traditions Hekate is associated with mortal crossings, both birth and death, and becomes a darker figure linked to magic and the dead. In Ovid's *Metamorphoses* (7. 234 ff.) Medea prays to Hekate and 'Youth' to release spirits of the dead. The internal story of Hekate within Greek mythology develops to associate her with the older, chthonic, deities who are often presented in opposition to the newer Olympian gods. The conflict between the older gods and the newer Olympian deities was the subject of the myth of the Gigantomachy, and a later aftershock is shown in Aeschylus' play *Eumenides*, where old and new forms of justice/vengeance come into conflict. In Valerius Flaccus' account of Jason's capture of the Golden Fleece, Medea is positioned squarely at that intersection between Hekate and the Olympian gods, as Hekate is sad to see Medea leave, and Venus boasts that Hekate is no match for her powers:

> Hecate's dismal powers
> are nothing for us to fear: let her appear or attempt
> to interfere with our purpose, and even she will feel pangs
> of passion stir for the *Argo*'s captain to whom we give aid.
>> (Valerius Flaccus, *Argonautica*
>> 7. 202–4, trans. Slavitt, 1999)

The imagery which surrounds Medea also links her to Hekate, as ideas of the moon, wild animals and torches are part of the iconography of both figures. Although it is not a topic to which our ancient sources pay much attention, we should not import ideas of the 'witch' as an old woman into our views of Medea. Specifically, we should note that in art Medea is shown as a beautiful young woman, not a wart-ridden hag. Although the ancient world did have strong ideas about the associations between moral goodness and physical beauty, Medea's status as granddaughter of Helios guaranteed her beauty, a fact which our reliance on literary sources can obscure. Furthermore, as a woman of marriageable age when she meets Jason in Kolchis, we should assume that Medea was somewhere between the ages of 14 and 19, the usual age for women to be married in most Greek cultures. Although she is an older married woman at the time of events in Korinth, she is certainly not in the category of 'old woman', but remains squarely in the age bracket of 'sexual and reproductive maturity' which most Greek societies viewed as particularly dangerous.

RITUAL

Medea's links to the divine sphere are undeniable, but these links are extrapolated mainly from narrative sources. These are the gods of myth, not necessarily of religion. If we turn to the sociohistorical background, we find that ritual practice was a cornerstone of Greek religious experience, and Medea's stories can be interpreted more directly in this context, as aetiological myths which explain the reasoning behind ritual practices. In this respect, her role in religion owes more to the position which she herself occupies on boundaries, rather than any clearly defined link to any particular god or goddess. Euripides makes his Medea the founder of the cult of Hera Akraia in Korinth, and other ancient sources explain the cult practices in Korinth as a ritual expiation for the death of Medea's children. She has been viewed as a foundation heroine, a mythological figure who prophesies or symbolises the establishment of a new community, an act requiring divine favour. This can be seen as part of a wider trend which links Medea to stories of initiation rituals. Such rituals were common in the Greek world, providing symbolic representations of the transitional stages in human life, such as childbirth or the assumption of adult status. The crossing of any boundary was seen as potentially dangerous, an idea still found in western society with the tradition of carrying a new bride over the threshold of a home – if she were to trip and fall bad luck would befall the marriage. Childbirth was a dangerous time for both the child and the mother, and the assumption of adult status in Greek societies often involved the idea of a test, if only symbolic, reinforcing the idea that being on a boundary makes an individual vulnerable to attack. The quest for the Golden Fleece may be a 'coming of age' rite of passage for Jason, which Medea facilitates. The link to childbirth places Medea at another crucial boundary, and her powers of rejuvenation imply the same dynamic. Graf has suggested that Medea's story may have originated in a context of initiation, but that she was then adopted by many Greek cultures who found her story useful in providing a story for their own rituals:

> If Medea can be plucked out of Panhellenic myth and used in ritual etiologies – rituals to which she might have had some original affinity, but from which, in general, she had distanced herself long ago – then this can only mean one thing: the mythmakers of the Greek archaic and classical periods were able to see (or rather sense) such affinities and to make them useful in new etiological narratives. When a pure story without any previous connection to a ritual lay before them, the general structure of the tale could suffice to hint at a ritual.
> (Graf, 1997, 42)

Throughout the artistic tradition, the ritual associations are evoked through ideas of sacrifice. The dismemberment of Apsyrtos is a perversion of ritual sacrifice, as is the death of Pelias, where ritual practice is deliberately left unfinished. In Euripides' *Medea* the chorus are warned to keep their distance when Medea murders the children with a formula from ritual sacrifice, intended to keep an action pure: 'He whose presence is not called for, let him absent himself from my sacrifices' (vv. 1053–5).

OVERVIEW

Medea emerges as a figure who functions on boundaries, representing fears about the limitations of human life. She is liminal, not only within her life story, moving between different cultures and societies, and disrupting the life patterns of other families, but also on an existential level, positioned between mortal and divine. She moves between different categories, at times the dangerous witch, at times the mother, understanding the pull which children exert, yet able to resist it. She is sometimes a violent figure with divine powers, yet is subject to many of the vicissitudes of human life – she struggles with family relationships and has nowhere to call home. To call her simply a 'witch' is to underestimate the complexities of her mythic persona. While many of these complexities derive from the diverse sources and variants, there is also a paradox inherent in all of her stories. She represents different modes of thought and action at one and the same time. For example, the betrayal by Jason which causes her to kill her children happens because she is situated in a mortal relationship as a woman, subject to male power, but her reaction transgresses the social boundaries. She employs a degree of violence, and a range of magical forces, which would not be available to the average woman in her situation. Even as a 'witch', Medea cannot be easily pigeonholed into any one category of magical figure: she is linked to a range of ideas, from the use of herbs, to the power of words, and has affinities with both the Olympian gods and the older, chthonic deities.

The discussions in this chapter have indicated the range of inter-related ideas contributing to the figure of the witch, particularly those concerning mortality. In the next chapter we will look at a related range of issues, which are more closely linked to the idea of the individual and his/her role in society.

5

ETHNICITY, GENDER
AND PHILOSOPHY

From issues of storytelling and the construction of reality, we now
move to a range of issues which have a more specific context in the
historical societies of ancient Greece. Medea's story fits into overlap-
ping areas of debate, particularly those connected with the definition
of identity. Greek societies commonly defined the role of 'adult'
through the sorts of binary oppositions we discussed in Chapter 3.
The citizen was specifically Greek not foreign, male not female, free
not enslaved. We saw in the previous chapter how Medea is often
positioned on conceptual borders, and this is true of her status as
a foreign woman who nonetheless exerts a masculine power in
Greek contexts. These two issues were central to the social aspects of
identity, but Medea's own attitude towards her situation brings in
a further issue, something which a modern audience might refer to
as the formation of a psychological identity. Medea, 'She who plans',
is sometimes presented as self-conscious about the contradictions of
story, ambivalent about her role in society, and engaged in an internal
debate which reflects the external debates she inspires around her.
In this chapter we will therefore be exploring fundamental issues of
self-image within Greek society, extending into a more philosophical
consideration of what it is to be human.

ETHNICITY

Fear of outsiders is one aspect of Medea's story which can be studied with a number of the approaches already mentioned. In a structuralist analysis, Medea is the foreigner who comes into the Greek world and disrupts the division of Greeks and non-Greeks. The figure of the witch throughout history has also been centred around a discourse of alienation. Fear of the unknown can lead to the demonisation of certain elements of society, and witches have traditionally been linked with places or ethnicities different from the dominant culture. Witches were traditionally associated in the ancient world with specific locations, such as Thessaly and Asia, areas on the edge of the known world. In later societies, witchcraft could be located in liminal spaces, such as the blasted heath in Shakespeare's *Macbeth*, or somewhere entirely imaginary. This spatial identification can be seen as a physical delineation of a psychological crisis – that which cannot be easily accommodated in the psyche is physically removed to a distant place. Kolchis is at the edge of the world in early myth; Mimnermus (fr. 11a) says that the city of Aietes is on the border of the Ocean, the great river which was believed to encircle the world, and thus marked its outer limits. This area of the world was known to the Greeks in the archaic period via trade links, and was a fertile site for the exchange of material, cultures and stories. It was, however, not a well-known geographical area, and fear of the unknown was a powerful force. Transferring this motif to the people of Kolchis, Diodorus Siculus 4. 46 gives a version of the story whereby Aietes puts to death all foreigners, and Medea as priestess of Artemis is charged with this task, but tries to save strangers, a similar motif to that found in Euripides' play *Iphigeneia in Tauris* where Iphigeneia is also the priestess of Artemis. This story type gives matching reasons for ethnic hostility: the Greeks are afraid because the foreigners will kill them, but the 'foreigners' perceive the Greeks as dangerous.

The attempt to create a structure for understanding outsiders, and find a place for them in one's own mental map, can be seen in the links made between Medea and the Medes. Herodotus *Histories* 7.6.2 says that the Arians changed their name to Medes 'when the Kolchian woman Medea came from Athens', and Hesiod refers to 'the great destiny' of Medea's son Medeios. For this purpose it does not make a great deal of difference whether Medeios is the child of Jason or of Aigeus, although in other stories of mythological descent ancestry can be highly significant. Links between Athens and other cultures were particularly complex because Athenians cherished the belief that they themselves were autochthonous, sprung from the very soil of Attica.

In the Greek world, the discourse of ethnicity was central to the creation of identity. While individuals were fiercely loyal to their city state, there was also a clear distinction of them and us, Greeks and non-Greeks. Euripides' play not only emphasises issues about men versus women, but also emphasises and distorts the issue of boundaries *per se*. Jason tells Medea that she is lucky to be living in the Greek world, demonstrating the Greek belief in their cultural superiority, but Medea pours scorn on his 'Greek' behaviour as fundamentally immoral. When the play was first produced in 431 BC it was only twenty years since Athens had enacted a law restricting citizenship. The Periclean citizenship law of 451 BC stated that a child could only be considered an Athenian citizen if his father and his mother were of Athenian citizen birth. This law made foreign wives less desirable, and made the idea of 'non-Athenian' as important as 'non-Greek'. In this context, Medea's cry that Jason is embarrassed to have a foreign wife (vv. 591–2) had a particular contemporary resonance.

It is interesting to note that this issue of ethnic identity, which could have such specific Greek and Athenian implications, is also one of the strongest themes in modern treatments of the myth, as we will see in Chapter 9.

GENDER

Previous sections have alluded to the fact that Medea's gender is central to her status as mythological figure, be it through structuralist analyses which figure women as 'the other', or through links to the processes of reproduction. This section will attempt to draw some of these strands together, and indicate how we can read the figure of Medea in ways which are, and are not, 'gender-neutral'. This term refers to interpretations which seek to make explicit the ideas about men and women which are operating within a text or discussion, particularly when trying to correct biases in previous scholarship. Readings of myth in the western tradition have been overwhelmingly dominated by men, and have worked with ideas about male/female interaction in which masculine values were equated with far more positive ideas than were female ones.

One important distinction of terminology is worth outlining before we proceed with this discussion. In the discourse of male/female relationships there is often a confusion of terms – an individual's 'sex' is not the same as his or her 'gender', although there are many discourses which assume that the two are synonymous. The distinction can be drawn as follows: an individual's 'sex' is the biological category referring to reproductive capacity; 'gender' is the package of attributes and behaviours which a society normally attaches to the reproductive capacity, but which are not tied to it in any natural or inevitable fashion. So, in modern British society the fact that male babies traditionally wear blue, whereas female babies wear pink, is an indication of gendering – there is no natural basis for the assignation of colours. In Medea's case, her sex is 'female', as she is biologically capable of giving birth, and she conforms to many of the patterns of behaviour which would gender her 'feminine'. However, her actions in taking violent revenge are more commonly associated with the masculine gender, so once again she provides an example of the problems of negotiating identity, of where to draw boundaries.

Throughout her story it is her dealings with men which are central, although in many accounts she does have a sister, Chalkiope. Valerius Flaccus' *Argonautica* (8. 140 ff.) also contains a moving scene in which Medea's flight is lamented by the women of the Kolchian house, and Medea's mother cries out to stop her. In an account relayed by Pausanias, Medea bears Jason a daughter called Eriopis, in addition to a son, Medeios (Pausanias 2.3.9 = Kinaethon fr. 2). The account of Eumelos via Pausanias that Medea turned down Zeus' advances out of respect for Hera implies an ability to form female bonds. However, in Euripides' play the manner in which she kills the young princess exploits what might be seen as female weaknesses, playing on the attraction of the children and the gift of an expensive dress.

Although she exists in a tradition of strong female figures, it is in relation to men that her strength is most commonly revealed. Medea can be viewed as a figure who represents the fearful 'other'. In patriarchal societies, it is common to define the dominant culture of masculinity by a process of exclusion. Just as light cannot be understood without the concept of dark, so male is defined negatively as 'not female'. This psychological move not only relegates the female to a secondary position, it attaches all sorts of negative connotations: if men are to be defined as strong and courageous, women must be defined as weak and cowardly. The artificiality of such divisions cannot be entirely ignored, and in a society where women are repressed it is common to find a male fear of women. Certainly in the ancient Greek world there was a concern about women breaking out and doing terrible things. Women were often associated with the dangers of nature and the wild, and images associated with marriage often play with this: the Athenian formula for marriage was to 'tame a woman for the ploughing of legitimate children'. In such a context, where male and female roles are sharply distinguished, the very fact that a woman in myth is female means that the story starts with certain assumptions and value judgements. The question posed at the start of this volume, 'Does it matter that Medea is a woman?', can easily be answered with a definite 'Yes'. This focus on women as 'the other' appears in several aspects of Medea's story which seem to challenge assumptions about women. Euripides' version is particularly striking, for his Medea appears to give a dispassionate view of women's capabilities: 'Women are fearful about everything, cowardly in the face of battle or the sword, but when they are insulted in matters of love, nothing is more bloodthirsty than a woman' (*Medea* vv. 263–6).

Many analyses of Medea have concentrated on her status as a female icon, but space constrains me to outline here just the major aspects which may not be indicated in other parts of this volume.

THE VOICE OF THE ACTOR

The world of ancient drama was male-dominated, and in Greek society was exclusively male. The actors, producers, and most, if not all, of the original audiences for Athenian tragedy and comedy were male, so when we look at the creation of a strong female figure, such as Euripides' Medea, we should not forget that 'she' is still a male creation. In classical Athens women were not allowed to perform in public, nor were they allowed to speak for themselves in legal cases. On the other hand, it was widely believed that women were in fact skilled performers who could disguise their intentions and deceive those around them, as does Klytaimestra in Aeschylus' *Agamemnon*. As often in the ancient world, a skill which could be praiseworthy in a man would be seen as a negative characteristic in a woman. Medea is a figure who is consistently presented as a consummate actor: in *Pythian* 4 Pindar gives Medea a voice and control of the action. As Braswell (1988) outlines, Pindar the narrator takes a step back and Medea becomes the director of events. Similarly, in Euripides' play Medea is able to assume different roles to achieve her end, as when she persuades Creon that she is powerless and vulnerable, only to switch back to her dominant position as soon as she has achieved a concession from him (vv. 364 ff.).

Medea the actor, as Zerba (2002) argues, is always playing a role, conscious of her self-presentation, and Erasmo (2004, 123–4) has argued that in Seneca's play Medea is the director of the action, conscious that Jason is her audience. Throughout her life story Medea controls events, particularly via her voice, from the magical intent of incantations, to the more rhetorical skills of persuasion, a talent shared by her aunt Kirke. One of the Greek terms for a practitioner of magic was '*goês*', or '*goêtês*', which meant literally 'a wailer', a reference to the power of language to achieve supernatural feats. Women were traditionally associated with lamentation, but Medea actually causes the lamentation of others. The opposition between male and female is complicated in this respect because Jason is traditionally portrayed as a good speaker, relying on his powers of rhetoric rather than brute force to achieve his aims. The relationship between Jason and Medea can thus be constructed as an opposition between different modes of speech and communication.

To a modern audience, Medea's self-presentation brings in ideas about gender, particularly those of Judith Butler (1990) on gender performativity, the idea that gender is something we play as a part.

Although this is a modern idea, there is an ancient parallel, which is the concept of dramatic performance; long before Athenian tragedy, Dionysos was associated with the transformation of gender. Initiation rites for adulthood across the Greek world often involved the temporary assumption of female dress, before a boy cast this off and assumed his male identity. Ancient drama has also been described by some as essentially feminine in nature, as it involves playing roles and transcending the normal codes of social behaviour.

FEMINIST READINGS

At its fundamental level feminism calls for an awareness of the artificiality of gender constructs, and an awareness that we live in a patriarchal society that continues to be dominated by men. Viewed from this broad perspective, many approaches could be termed 'feminist', although they might not explicitly accept this label. Once we move on from this set of first principles, we find a multitude of different 'feminist' approaches which may conflict with each other, and raise different questions. For example, when a man writes about Medea today, what does he bring to it? Is it important to know that commentators such as Hunter, Elliott, or Mastronarde are men? Can any of them claim to understand Medea, or are they irremediably addled by testosterone (as female critics of an earlier generation were seen to be limited by their hormones)? Do I as a woman have any particular claim to be able to understand Medea (based on ideas of lived experience), or have I abandoned my female perspective by choosing to live and work in the male-dominated culture of academia? If language is essentially a male tool in a male-dominated society, can I ever say anything from an authentic female perspective? The study of the classical world has traditionally been a male preserve, so we need to be aware of the force of tradition (see Rabinowitz and Richlin, 1993). In this section we will examine attempts to counter the dominant perceptions of the patriarchal society.

An example will indicate the sorts of problems we can address with an awareness of gender issues. Let us consider a passage from Euripides' *Medea*, a section from the messenger speech describing how the daughter of Creon reacted with delight to the gifts Medea had sent, unaware of the fact that they will lead to her death (vv. 1163–70):

> Then up she jumped from her dressing-table
> And prinked around the room on her little white feet,
> Glorying in her presents, again and again,
> Posing, checking from head to heel.
> Then, all of a sudden, something dreadful.
> She changed colour, staggered,
> Started to shiver, managed just
> To fall on the bed, not on the floor.
>
> (trans. Walton and Thompson, 2000)

The line Walton translates as 'Posing, checking from head to heel' says literally in the Greek something like 'looked at her stretched tendon', generally taken to be a reference to the Achilles' tendon. It is interesting to note that in his commentary on this passage Alan Elliott (1969) shows some awareness of the issue of gender with the remark, 'Years of discussion by scholarly males, some of them bachelors, have not produced an agreed answer to the question, "What is she actually doing?" The most natural suggestion is that she is pointing her toe and looking at the fall of the dress to her side or behind her' (Elliott, 1969, 96). Although this remark seems to indicate an awareness of gender bias, it is not gender-neutral; it implies that Elliott as a married man (as stated in the acknowledgements, p. 140) has greater insight into the female mind or patterns of behaviour than did earlier unmarried critics. This might sound like a reasonable proposition, but many would argue that marriage is a patriarchal institution which controls women, and that any understanding of women which a man might gain from marriage is ultimately flawed and partial. Furthermore, the assertion that marriage gives a man a greater understanding of women's behaviour is part of a framework in which men control women, and understanding their behaviour is simply another tool for the coercion of women. In many ways this remains an excellent commentary for those reading the play in Greek, but it is ironic that a male critic should proudly parade his married status as giving him greater insight into Medea's situation.

Feminist approaches to the story start with an idea that Medea was damned because of characteristics which ancient society disapproved of in a woman, and that this gender dynamic was in operation before any crimes were committed. As a clever, resourceful woman she was bound to inspire ill-feeling. There are a number of readings of Medea which choose to reinterpret her in a positive light. Cahill (1995) retells the myth and lessens the stain of murder by suggesting that Medea can in fact rejuvenate her children. Other readings emphasise Medea's status as victim rather than villain: Christa Wolf's version proposes that she had no choice, that in the rigid confines of a male-dominated society her only reasonable option was to kill the children. Although such views may help us to see more clearly the underlying assumptions which we often bring to texts, we should be careful in applying such readings; we do not want simply to reverse the opposition, so that 'Women Bad, Men Good' is automatically corrected to 'Women Good, Men Bad', an equally distorted view of gender relationships.

Other interpretations of the myth emphasise the patriarchal structures which contain Medea, and understand her actions as transgressions of male codes of conduct. The fact that patriarchal societies have traditionally given men power leads to an unspoken view that men are associated with all that is good, honourable and beautiful. Therefore, any challenge to male institutions is automatically un-good, un-honourable, un-beautiful (to borrow an idea from George Orwell). If we challenge the moral superiority of those male codes, Medea can be seen as a more positive figure. Instead of focusing on Medea as a helper-maiden whose skill and intelligence are suspect, we can instead see her as a hero in her own right, and praise her talents just as we would were she a man. Such an approach is suggested in Euripides' play when the chorus challenge the male traditions of poetry which cast women in a bad light (vv. 1081 ff.).

Certainly women throughout myth and history could claim that they have been denied a voice and a fair hearing, but Medea is not so easily rehabilitated as a female icon. Even if we move away from a patriarchal society, the act of killing one's children is likely to remain morally abhorrent, however much women assert their own voices. This is the point at which we need to remember other versions of the story in which Medea is not directly responsible. Just as the Korinthians were said to have bribed Euripides to take the blame off them, we could say that the stain of infanticide on Medea's character is an imposition by a male society on a female figure who was originally more positive. Some have argued for strong traditions of early matrilineal societies, and Maitland (1992) discussed tragic myths in relation to this idea, but concludes that the evidence for such a scenario is slight.

We return to the idea of male fear of women. Just as childbirth can create demons, so society can create fear of women. Medea's characteristics, use of magic, wisdom, power, etc. can be seen as neutral until they fall under a male-dominated schema which says that for male to be good, female must be bad. As a figure who displays male and female characteristics Medea is 'good to think with'; she poses questions without providing easy answers. But as the next section will demonstrate, Medea can be shown as 'good to think with' in more abstract terms as well.

PHILOSOPHICAL CONSIDERATIONS

Just as Medea's story can raise issues of nationality and gendered identity, so it can be used to explore problems of mental conflict within an individual. In Euripides' play we see a vivid dramatisation of the dilemma facing Medea, as she eventually chooses to kill her children to take revenge on Jason. The conflict is vocalised (vv. 1019 ff.) as Medea struggles to decide between her love of her children and her desire for revenge, concluding at v. 1079 with the line 'Passion is stronger than my reason' (passion = the Greek *thumos*, reason = the Greek *bouleumata*, which can also be translated 'plans'). Although there is considerable controversy about lines 1055–80, which some have thought are interpolated because of difficulties of vocabulary and staging, these lines have certainly been influential in antiquity and today.

Medea's conflict is used as an example of various philosophical ideas about decision making (see Dillon, 1990). It can demonstrate the concept of *akrasia*, lack of self-discipline, and was taken up by many ancient philosophers in their discussion of how the mind deals with conflicting desires, not least in the Platonic schema of the tripartite

division of the soul. Medea's links to Hekate also associate her with later philosophical, religious thinking as Hekate's role in the Chaldean Oracles associates her with the figure of the Cosmic Soul (see Johnston, 1990). The Chaldean Oracles are a collection of information about theological, cosmological and ritual practices written in dactylic hexameters. They are said to have been written down by Julian 'The Theurgist' in the second century AD, so they are a late addition to the mythological corpus; but they give Hekate a central role as an intermediary between different worlds, an interesting link with Medea's position on the mortal/immortal boundary. Also in later traditions, as in Seneca's play, Medea can be seen in a Stoic analysis as the embodiment of the irrational passions which need to be controlled. Newman (2001) has argued that this tradition goes back to the earliest stories: 'Euripides' *Medea*, then, is about a primitive dragon spirit who impinges on Greek rationality, estranging its sanitized world' (p. 58). On this reading, Medea is seen as an almost-allegorical figure, created by associations with snakes, sun gods and the female.

These connections may well be relevant on some level, but the fact that interests me about the philosophical perspective is that these debates, which are of utmost importance to the philosophical enterprise, can be illustrated with reference to a *female* mythological character. It is not the same as when fourth-century BC orators quote from female figures in tragedy to illustrate their points. Rather, there seems to be a basic concept that women have complex mental processes, which goes against the Aristotelian view expressed most strongly in *Generation of Animals* that women are undeveloped men, and thus by nature subordinate to the greater rational powers of men. One source of the myth suggested that perhaps ancient generalisations about the inferior mental powers of women were false. Names were highly significant in the ancient world, and it is surely no coincidence that the name Medea, connected to the Greek verb meaning 'to contemplate, plot or plan', should be associated with debates about the control of the mind itself.

OVERVIEW

Medea is certainly not the average Greek individual, and yet because she demonstrates behaviours and characteristics which Greek society deems excessive and undesirable, we can form a better understanding of the norms and values of that society. At the same time, her story constantly challenges comfortable assumptions that we can draw neat distinctions between what is and what is not acceptable. Greek superiority over barbarians may be confirmed by thinking of Medea as an uncivilised foreigner who commits terrible crimes, but her ability to outwit many Greeks in many contexts suggests some areas in which the barbarians may have the advantage. Similar patterns can be observed in the gender dynamics within the myth. When these social paradoxes are combined with the philosophical aspects of Medea's own struggle for self-determination, we are presented with a set of stories which function on many levels and relate to many of the fundamental questions of self-definition which were posed in ancient societies, and which are still relevant today.

6

EURIPIDES' VERSION OF MYTH

In the previous chapters we have discussed the malleability of myth, and noted the ways in which several different versions of Medea's story coexisted in the Greek world. In this chapter we will discuss a turning point in the development of the myth, the emergence of one variant which would come to overshadow all other accounts of Medea in the Graeco-Roman world.

MEDEA IN TRAGEDY

Several episodes in Medea's life were dramatised in fifth-century Athens. Tragedy was staged as part of Athens' annual spring worship of the god Dionysos at the festival of the City Dionysia. Three play-wrights were chosen to present three tragedies each followed by a satyr play. The playwrights were in competition, which encouraged a lively interaction with mythological material as each strove to impress the audience with his command of the stories. Of the many plays that featured Medea as a character, only one has survived, Euripides' *Medea*, produced in 431 BC. However, from fragments and hypotheses we know of several other plays which are relevant to the development of the myth. Aeschylus' play *Nurses of Dionysos* seems to have referred to Medea's magical rejuvenation of the old women as a favour to Dionysos. We should note that this early play probably reflects the dominant artistic tradition, focused on the Pelias episode. Similarly, Sophocles' play *Rhizotomoi* (Root-cutters) is generally believed to have

been about Medea as a magical figure, the title referring to her production of potions from plants. His *Kolchian Women* also centred around Medea's natal household. In 455 BC Euripides presented *Peliades* (Daughters of Pelias), telling of the death of Pelias at Medea's hands, and both Sophocles and Euripides produced plays entitled *Aigeus* which may well have featured Medea's arrival in Athens, or her later attempt to kill Theseus when he came to acknowledge his father. The loss of these plays prevents us from gaining a full understanding of the role of Medea as a tragic heroine, but it seems unlikely that there was a single, stereotypical image of Medea in fifth-century Athens.

EURIPIDES' MEDEA

The play is set in Korinth, where Jason and Medea have sought refuge with their two sons after the murder of Pelias. As the play opens we hear from Medea's nurse that Jason has married the princess of Korinth, and that Medea is devastated. As the play progresses we see Medea determine to take her revenge on Jason, deciding that the only way to hurt him as he has hurt her is to kill their children. Although she agonises over the decision, Medea does eventually kill her sons, as well as Jason's new bride. The play closes as Medea takes the bodies of her sons in the chariot of her grandfather, Helios. She will go to Athens where she has been promised asylum by King Aigeus, and she leaves Jason with a prophecy that he will live out his life alone, finally to be killed by a beam falling from the rotting hull of his ship, the *Argo*.

Female characterisation

From the first scene of the play we are aware that this Medea is a dangerous figure. Her nurse speaks of the violence of her grief, and fears that Medea may turn her anger against the children. Her fears are increased as we hear Medea's cries from off stage (vv. 112–14, 'I hate you children of a hated mother. Curses on you and your father'). We also are reminded of an earlier episode in the story, Medea's murder of her brother Apsyrtos, as she calls attention to the crimes she

committed on Jason's behalf (vv. 166–7). The violence of Medea's character is a constant feature in this play. She herself highlights this, claiming that all women have the capacity for violence when they are slighted in matters of the heart (vv. 256–60).

Medea's willingness to use physical means to gain her revenge would have been seen as a male trait by the Athenian audience, as their society endorsed rigid stereotypes of masculine and feminine behaviours, and women were believed to be vulnerable and weak. The use of magic and poison in the murder of the princess would have been seen as a feminine trait, but in Euripides' play Medea combines this female source of power with masculine, physical power. Her initial thoughts on how to take her revenge are openly aggressive, 'Shall I sneak in and set fire to the bed or stab them?' (vv. 376–85), and she eventually kills her sons with a sword.

The masculine/feminine dichotomy is fundamental to Euripides' portrayal of his central character. Initially she is presented as a character obsessed by female concerns: Jason sneers at her, 'You women are all alike, obsessed with sex' (vv. 569–73). Medea's ability to deceive and manipulate those around her would also have been viewed as a negative female trait by the Athenian audience. She is presented as having a strong maternal love for her sons, dwelling on the physical connection between a mother and her children (vv. 1069–75). On the other hand, she is able to kill her sons, denying the traditional place of women in Greek society as the natural carers for children. Her action is so horrific that the chorus of women, who had previously supported her, now turn against her. When they try to find a parallel for her situation they cannot, indicating how shocking was her crime. The only comparison they can draw is with Ino, who killed her own children by mistake (vv. 1282–8). Even though the chorus members themselves earlier expressed dissatisfaction with the joys of having children (vv. 1081–115), Medea's actions are extreme, a denial of feminine identity. Some scholars have even claimed that Medea destroys her status as a woman when she destroys her children.

As a counterpoint to this highly feminised portrayal, Euripides presents Medea as possessing male traits of physical violence and high intelligence. Kreon, the king of Korinth, decides to banish Medea because of her intellect. He tells her, 'You're a clever woman, and I'm afraid of you' (vv. 282–91). For a Greek audience, excessive intelligence in a woman was not just a bad thing, but unnatural. (Aristotle, *Politics* 1254 b 10–14, gives a succinct account of the belief that men had a natural superiority over women because of greater intelligence, just as humans had greater intelligence than animals.) Euripides' play presents a Medea who possesses both male and female characteristics, and is all the more dangerous because of it. In a society where gender roles were prescribed and restrictive, a character who stepped outside the boundaries of accepted behaviour for his or her gender was condemned and feared. This fact alone meant that for the Athenian audience Euripides' character was intrinsically a dangerous woman, regardless of her previous actions or her plan of revenge on Jason.

We should note that the truth of gender stereotypes is challenged in the play, as the chorus of Korinthian women also behave in ways which the audience might have found unfeminine. They support Medea's desire for revenge, even when she plans to kill Jason and the princess, and they talk with anxiety about the ambiguity of the assumed female satisfactions of having children (vv. 1081 ff.). The choruswomen protest that women have been unfairly treated by poets (vv. 416–30) and agree with Medea when she makes her famous assertion, 'I would rather stand three times in the line of battle than bear one child' (vv. 250–1). This statement has often been used as a starting point for feminist readings of Greek tragedy and culture, as it directly confronts one of the defining ideologies of gender relations in the Greek world: male identity was created through participation in warfare, female identity through the process of marriage and child-birth. Men were seen as the protectors, women as the protected, so Medea's assertion of the relative dangers of war and childbirth is a direct challenge to that idea.

However, before we take this statement as an indication that Euripides was presenting Medea as a proto-feminist, we should remember the context of the remark, both within the play and within Athenian society. In the play Medea's assertion of the trials of womanhood forms part of her attempt to gain the chorus' sympathy and their acquiescence to her plans. As with many of her remarks throughout the play, we should not take it at face value, but rather understand it as a deliberate attempt to manipulate and deceive. There is a paradox that as she elicits sympathy for women's lot, she also displays one of the characteristic behaviours, deceit, which formed part of the negative Greek stereotype of women. In this wider context, we should also remember that the audience of Greek tragedy was predominantly, if not exclusively, male and part of a society which valued men far more highly than women. It is certainly true that childbirth was a dangerous business in the ancient world, but for a woman to assert that it was three times more dangerous than taking part in warfare would have been seen as absurd. Furthermore, her remark may well have been taken as insulting. Greek masculinity was based around military prowess and glory, so the denigration of such activity in comparison to childbirth was shocking. Modern audiences may receive Medea's comments as a positive rallying cry, but the original audience members were probably shocked, even offended, and their views of Medea may have become hardened and hostile at this early point in the drama, colouring their response to the whole of the play.

Mortality and divinity

To this point, we have been exploring the character of Medea as a mortal woman, an interpretation which she herself promotes as she tries to ally herself to the chorus of Korinthian women, and to dispel Kreon's fears. However, Medea's mortality is open to question in this play. We have seen that in previous versions of the myth, Medea's divine genealogy figured prominently. As granddaughter of Helios she belongs to a family with many magical powers. Her father employed powers more than mortal in attempting to stop Jason stealing the Golden Fleece, and Medea's aid to Jason was also magical.

Euripides' version adds an extra layer of complexity to the myth as the play explores the boundaries between mortal and immortal. The liminality of Medea's character will be a strong focus in later versions of the myth, and Euripides' play is where this development first appears explicitly. One of the striking features of Medea's male/female persona in the play is that she displays the traits of both genders *to an extreme*. The excesses of her character can be seen as a mark of divinity, as gods are presented in Greek religion as taking mortal characteristics to extremes. Furthermore, the ability of one character to be both masculine and feminine could be read in the ancient world as something unnatural, to the extent that it could be taken as indicative of divinity. In modern societies, we are increasingly open to the idea that gender boundaries are to some extent artificial creations of society, as we discussed in Chapter 5. In fifth-century Athens, the gender boundaries were supposed to be natural, and thus anyone who could break them as confidently as Medea would be seen as unnatural and verging on the divine.

Medea's divine powers in this play are largely hidden at the start by Medea herself. It is only as the play progresses that we see more of her family background, as she has the means to poison a dress and thus kill the princess, and finally she is rescued by her grandfather, the sun god, Helios. It is noteworthy that the only successfully supportive family relationship depicted in the play is that between Medea and her grandfather, and the final scene of the play forces the audience to contemplate whether Medea was ever the helpless mortal she has claimed to be. Her high intelligence, her ability to combine male and female traits, her willingness to sacrifice personal attachments in order to achieve revenge could all be understood by an ancient audience as indications that Medea was not mortal. One of the great contributions made by Euripides to the evolution of the myth was to provide such a powerful example of how mortality and divinity need not be directly opposed to each other, as binary opposites in a structuralist model, but could be seen as the extremes of a continuum.

A further aspect of this mortal/divine interaction is the problem of justice which is raised at the end of the play. Medea claims that Jason hasn't a leg to stand on when he calls for vengeance, because he has broken his oath of marriage (v. 1391). This was not an ordinary contract of marriage which could be dissolved, as in Athenian practice. It was a formal oath of loyalty which Jason swore to Medea when he took her from Kolchis, and was therefore overseen by Zeus himself in his role as Zeus Horkios (Zeus of Oaths). Medea presents herself as the agent of Zeus' revenge on Jason, a Fury acting as a divine figure, rather than a mortal woman seeking personal revenge. Medea tells Jason that she will be a 'curse' on his household (v. 608), and the chorus say that there is a 'fury' in the house (v. 1260). Jason, understandably, does not share this view of Medea's divine authorisation, and cries out at the end of the play that there will be vengeance for the murder of the children, that Medea in turn will be punished for her actions.

Here we see one of the most problematic and worrying aspects of Medea's mythology. Even though she commits many acts of violence which would have been condemned throughout the Greek world, she is never punished directly. She escapes from Kolchis after betraying her family and killing her brother; she escapes from Iolkos after tricking the daughters of Pelias into killing their father; she escapes from Korinth after the murder of the children; and she will escape from Athens after attempting to murder Theseus. This is an element of the story which the Roman poet Ovid explored with particular subtlety, as we will see in the next chapter, but it is the final scenes of Euripides' play which gives this problem its most powerful expression. Medea appears in the chariot of the sun god, placed high on the *mechane*, the stage crane which was used to bring gods on stage in fifth-century tragedy. This spatial alignment makes it clear that Medea is no longer a mortal, and raises the question of whether she ever truly was. The audience is left to contemplate two unpalatable conclusions as Medea escapes unpunished after committing the most terrible of crimes. Either Medea is divine, and the gods can come among us and exact revenge for our crimes with savage force; or Medea is mortal, and sometimes mortal crimes go unpunished.

It has sometimes been said that the message or force of Euripides' play comes in its warning that mortal women are powerful, and can react badly when slighted. However, it is doubtful whether the original audience would have viewed Medea as a simple mortal figure, interpreting her story as one of simple human equations. Certainly the story could be understood as containing hidden warnings about male/female interactions, but the more interesting focus is the inter-action between gods and mortals.

This play actively explores the contradictions inherent in the mythology of Medea and provides no simple answers. Euripides' char-acter may be mortal, immortal or something in between, depending on which section of the play we are considering, just as she appears by turns essentially female or male in her behaviour. It could be seen as Euripides' greatest achievement, to take a complex figure from Greek myth and to encapsulate all of those complicated and often contradictory qualities within one dramatic character. In the final section of this chapter we will look in more detail at the process of *mythopoesis*, the constant reinvention of myth which Euripides employed, and the problems of presenting Medea's story to an Athenian audience. To close this discussion of her characterisation in the play we shall look at the issue of consistency, and ask whether Euripides has managed to pin down the essence of the myth of Medea.

Consistency

In his discussion of the ideal tragedy in *The Poetics* (1454 b) Aristotle cautioned playwrights that their characters should be consistent. The Greek word 'character' means literally a stamp or a brand, and implies that your character is something fixed about you. Indeed, it was a legitimate line of defence in Greek law to marshal enough character witnesses to swear you could not have committed an alleged offence because that would be incompatible with your known stable character, a principle we see in the defence speech composed by Antiphon, *On the Murder of Herodes*. Philosophers such as Plato and Aristotle argued that character could be changed for the better or for the worse, but the common-sense view seems to have been that you were what you were.

While some scholars, such as Burnett (1973) and Knox (1977), have argued that Medea is consistent in pursuing a heroic model of revenge, others have argued that even a cursory reading of Euripides' *Medea* might indicate that Euripides has not created a consistent character: Medea expresses a number of contradictory views, and is shown engaging in a violent internal debate as she resolves to kill her children. At the start of the play we have just heard Medea's impassioned cries of grief from off stage when she appears calm, and in control of a rational argument, manipulating the choruswomen. At the end of the play we see a character who is far more detached and powerful than the Medea of earlier scenes. Before we condemn Euripides as an incompetent playwright, we should return to Aristotle's words, for he continues to say that if consistency is not possible, the character should be 'consistently inconsistent'. This is one way in which we could interpret Euripides' figure. She is changeable and unpredictable, such that even Jason, who is presumed to have known her the longest, does not foresee the danger she poses. Her good friend Aigeus similarly does not realise the full extent of her planned revenge, and Kreon, who does have some insight, still thinks she cannot do anything in a single day. Medea's ability to frustrate the expectations of those around her may be one aspect of her divinity, and thus this pattern gives a certain consistency to her character.

We can, however, take the argument further and explore the ways in which Euripides has created his figure with reference to the earlier myths. There have been a number of recent studies of this play which have emphasised the difficulties of defining her character. For our purposes, two of these approaches are most helpful as they indicate how Euripides was responding to, and shaping, the evolving myth of Medea.

Boedeker (1997) has argued that part of the problem for an audience trying to understand the character of Medea in this play is that the other characters are unsuccessful in their own attempts to define her. In her analysis of the play, Boedeker outlines a pattern by which the other characters try to find appropriate imagery with which to describe Medea, ranging from animal imagery (Medea as a lioness, v. 189) to comparisons with inanimate objects such as rocks or the sea (vv. 27–9), or to Jason's final cries that Medea is a mythological monster, 'worse than Skylla' (vv. 1132–3). Medea herself never conforms to any of the patterns suggested, and so remains an elusive figure in a vortex of images, far more so than other female figures such as Antigone or Klytaimestra whose stories can raise similar issues. On related lines, Sourvinou-Inwood (1997) argues that Medea is constantly reinterpreted in relation to different schemata of 'the good woman', 'the bad woman', 'the normal woman', and never consistently conforms to any of the structures Greek society would seek to impose on her.

These lines of interpretation are relevant for our attempts to understand how Euripides responded to the mythological tradition as he inherited it. The technique of dramatic composition has the effect of disorientating an audience, and so has a particular purpose.

However, it can also be seen as a sophisticated response to the mythology of Medea, an attempt to crystallise her figure, not by pinning her down in acts of description, but by accepting the chaos. Euripides may have understood that the myth of Medea was not to be understood or appreciated by simple structures or descriptions. To grasp the meaning of the myth was to accept that the standard tools of interpretation and circumscription which humans apply to the world are not always adequate, that sometimes we have to accept that we will not understand, that the contradictions inherent in the myth of Medea cannot be reconciled, they can only be accepted. Thus, the application of a particular method of dramatic composition may indicate a wider process of philosophical enquiry into myth underlying the production of the play.

Medea the actor

There are, however, other ways of configuring the relationship between Euripides' Medea and her myth. Zerba (2002) suggests that the inconsistencies in Medea's character are most significant if read in the context of the theatre itself. The difficulties of pinning down Medea experienced by an audience mimic the difficulties experienced by the other characters. Medea is such an accomplished liar that no one, the audience members included, can be sure that they have ever seen the real Medea. It may be that the audience can only conclude with certainty that Medea is an expert manipulator.

This line of interpretation is widely accepted in classical scholarship, but Zerba takes the argument one stage further, suggesting that Medea is presented as the consummate actor, able to assume different parts at will. She argues that Medea's manipulation of those around her demonstrates a self-conscious 'actorly aplomb', as she assumes a range of different identities, just like an actor wearing different masks. Zerba suggests that in his Medea Euripides created the forerunner of Shakespearean protagonists such as Hamlet, who display a complex understanding of character and action. There is a strong correlation between the actions of Euripides the playwright and Medea the character, on Zerba's analysis, which forces the audience to contemplate the nature of drama and reality, a move which may be termed metatheatrical.[1] Thus we see the importance of interpreting context when we look at any version of a myth. It is not just the details of the story which are important; the medium of transmission is just as significant, particularly when dealing with a genre which was as self-conscious and innovative as Greek tragedy.

Medea and Athens

As the previous section has indicated, the status of Euripides' version as a piece of theatre intended for a specific audience is very important in determining the playwright's intentions and the way in which this play fitted into the evolution of the myth. The chapter will conclude, therefore, with a more detailed discussion of the place of the play in the Athenian theatrical tradition, and an analysis of what fifth-century Athenians made of the myth of Medea more widely.

We need to consider the place of Medea in the Greek, and specifically Athenian, imagination. The first question to address is what exactly Euripides did to the mythological tradition he inherited. Some scholars have argued that Euripides was the first to make Medea directly responsible for killing her children in an act of revenge for Jason's infidelity, an issue discussed by McDermott (1989, 9–24). Others, such as Michelini (1987), have argued that the innovation in this respect came from an earlier playwright, Neophron, and that Euripides was following a new variant rather than inventing it. For an excellent summary of the argument plus direct citation of the Neophron fragments see Mastronarde (2002, 57–64), who concludes it is more likely that Neophron wrote after Euripides' play, rather than vice versa.

Given the influence of Euripides' play over later generations, I think it is likely that it was his own invention, or that at the very least he was the first to bring out explicitly the ramifications of such a change. His Medea now develops a complex psychological persona, which throws a spotlight on fundamental relationships in human nature. Delving into the dark recesses of the human mind was a speciality of Euripides, and it is likely that much of the passion and vengeance which modern readers associate with Medea comes more from the nature of Euripidean drama than from any underlying 'meaning' to the myth.

But let us consider further the reasons for the failure of the play. Any number could be adduced, ranging from the quality of the other plays Euripides presented that year to the prevailing weather conditions on the day of the performance. It is possible that the Athenian audience was disturbed by the presentation of a powerful woman, or that they responded badly to the interplay of Greek and barbarian elements. Some scholars have argued that the original audience would not have related Medea's story directly to their own lives, as they would have viewed her as an uncivilised barbarian. Such are the views expressed by Page (1938) in his commentary on the play, remarks which may say more about his own colonial views than about the original performance conditions. However, many have argued, I believe correctly, that the original audience may well have been directly affected by the story, not just as Greeks, but as Athenians, a line forcefully argued by Knox (1977). Although Holland (2003) has recently argued that the focus of the story is the inherited curse on the Korinthian royal family, the House of Aiolos, there is constant reference to the Athenian perspective. Throughout the play Medea is treated by those around her as a Greek woman; even Jason tells her she is lucky to have become civilised. Although she herself calls attention when it suits her to her lack of status, she acts as if she has become thoroughly assimilated to Greek society. Furthermore, she is only one step away from becoming an honorary Athenian.

The role of Aigeus in the play was potentially the most disturbing element in the story for the Athenian audience. The king of Athens is shown as compassionate, but perhaps not wise. Sfyroeras (1994) has argued persuasively that Aigeus is like a 'surrogate audience member' in the play. By offering Medea a refuge in Athens, he gives her an escape route, and thus makes all of Athens complicit in the horrific murders that follow. This may have been seen as a sideswipe at the much-vaunted Athenian virtue of offering asylum to all comers, a perspective which was not likely to gain favour with the competition judges. The positive portrayal of Athens as a place of refuge can be seen in a number of sources, such as the late fifth-/early fourth-century writer Xenophon who, in his *Memories of Socrates* 3.5.10, calls Athens 'a sanctuary for victims of oppression'.

However, before we conclude that Euripides' Medea was a figure created from political and psychological problems for a particular audience alone, we must consider one final dimension, which brings in the issue of theatricality we discussed above in relation to Medea's character. Euripides' play is a visual feast which inspired a number of vase paintings showing Medea in the great chariot of the sun. One such painting is illustrated in Figure 3, an image we will discuss in the next chapter. This is a strong visual image which can compete with any of the great theatrical set pieces of earlier tragedians, such as Aeschylus' portrayal of Klytaimestra arriving on stage after the murder of her husband in *Agamemnon*. Euripides may have been trying to establish Medea as the 'worst of women', challenging the crown held in drama by Klytaimestra. The extremity of Medea in Euripides' play could be read as an attempt to outdo previous versions of female villainy, and change her position in the mythological hierarchy. We should never forget that the myths of an individual character did not exist in isolation, and could be influenced in a number of ways by other stories. Furthermore, considerations of dramatic necessity could also have a significant impact on the success of a story; Aristotle (*Rhetoric* 2.23.28) says that Karkinos wrote a tragedy, *Medea*, but failed to control the dramatic tension because the children were sent away during the course of the play.

OVERVIEW

In his handling of the myth, Euripides produced a complex but engaging portrayal of Medea which was influential over later generations because of its artistic strength and mythological subtlety. A wide range of issues is involved in his play, as questions of gender, ethnicity and mortality are shown to be interrelated, and no easy solutions to the great problems of life are offered. As a piece written for competition in a specific set of circumstances, the play tells us about the way the myth was received in fifth-century Athens. However, the long-lasting reputation of this one instantiation of the myth indicates that

Euripides understood something of the essential character of Medea's story, which justifies the extended treatment of the play provided here. In the next chapter we will see how the development of the myth owed a great deal to Euripides' version, and how this one episode came to be viewed as a microcosm of Medea's entire life story.

7

MYTH ABOUT MYTH: FROM GREECE TO ROME

We saw in the previous chapter how Euripides created a Medea with explicit motivations which would dominate later versions of her story. The jealous woman killing her children is the most prominent version of the story available in the early twenty-first century, but the years separating us from Euripides' play contain a startling series of metamorphoses in the myth of Medea. Western culture came to know Greek tragedy through the filter of Roman culture, so this chapter will explore some of the stages through which the myth passed.

Although this chapter will proceed in roughly chronological order, the intention is not to provide an account of the historical development of the figure of Medea. Rather, it is to show two things. First, by examining different artistic responses to the figure of Medea we gain a fuller appreciation of some of the key features we discussed in chapters 3 to 5, and the responses created by those who were working with the myth as a living process, rather than by those attempting to classify and systematise it many centuries later. Secondly, we will gain a better understanding of the material which forms the cultural backdrop to any modern understanding of Medea. In addition to establishing the contexts for the various representations from the Hellenistic world into the world of first-century Rome, we will see the reworking of two particular themes: the issue of metamorphosis and the relationship between language and rationality.

THE VISUAL TRADITION

We closed the previous chapter's discussion by noting the highly visual presentation of Euripides' heroine. The most immediate reaction to this instantiation of the myth, as far as we can tell, came in vase paintings which increasingly feature Medea in lurid scenes surrounding the death of her children. As we noted in chapter 2, the relationship between literature and artistic works in other media is difficult to gauge, but this does seem to be one occasion when a strong case can be made for the influence of a literary source on an exterior artistic tradition. One of the most striking images in the new repertoire is shown in figure 3, a Lucanian red-figure bell krater (mixing bowl) from around 400 BC. The bodies of Medea's sons are lying over an altar, and the chariot of the sun is centrepiece of the scene. Medea is completely cut off from the other figures, more closely linked to the figures of the Furies on either side of the vase. The bodies of the sons are displayed in graphic physicality, and Jason, standing on the left of the scene, is unable to engage at any level.

There has been much debate about the relationship between this image (and those like it) and Euripides' play, with many suggestions about iconographic conventions which tie this to a production of the play. However, we should also remember that plays other than Euripides' may have been produced, and that vases such as the one shown in figure 3 need not be seen as illustrations of drama. It is for our purposes a good indication that Medea in popular imagination was increasingly associated with the murder of her children. Sourvinou-Inwood (1997) provides an excellent summary of the iconographic tradition, arguing that there is a significant further aspect to the new scenes, namely that Medea now comes to be shown in specifically oriental dress, as she is in figure 3. Sourvinou-Inwood further links this vase directly to Euripides' play, and does not view the position of the sons on the altar as a significant divergence from that drama, in which the children are shown in the chariot itself. The position on the altar can be understood as an artistic signifier of the unholy nature of the act, a perversion of the ritual sacrifice which we noted as a touch of irony in Euripides' play itself.

Figure 3 Apulian red-figure volute krater, showing Medea in chariot escaping after the murder of her children, c. 340 BC.

Source: Image © The Cleveland Museum of Art.

There are a number of vases showing Medea in this sort of scene from the Greek colonies of southern Italy, where tragedy was enthusiastically received in the fourth century, and Euripides' plays were particularly popular. Even at this stage a version of the myth which, as we saw in the previous chapter, had a complex relationship with

Athens, could still travel widely. This is the same power of reimagination which takes the story from Greece to Rome.

APOLLONIOS RHODIOS

Western culture received its Greek mythology via Rome. In many cases there was a process of assimilation and mythological equivalency when Rome became the dominant culture in the Mediterranean. Figures such as Zeus or Herakles were equated with, or assimilated to, Jupiter and Hercules, and so on. In the case of Medea, however, there was no Roman equivalent, even though Smith (1999) has noted the wide spread of the myth in Italy. Medea remains an anomalous figure of myth representing Greek/Barbarian even within the Roman world, which frequently defined Roman versus Greek.

Roman culture acquired much of its knowledge of Greek mythology via the Hellenistic world (third century BC). One of the most valuable legacies of Alexander the Great was the foundation of the city of Alexandria on the coast of Egypt. From its beginnings in 331 BC, Alexandria quickly grew into a cosmopolitan city of culture. As the rest of the Mediterranean world experienced rapid fluctuations and power struggles, Alexandria cultivated a literary and artistic niche, supported by the patronage of the Ptolemies. The Library of Alexandria provided a centre of learning and the preservation of Greek culture, which was protected and used by a new generation of artists and writers. The so-called 'Hellenistic' poets, such as Kallimachos, were highly educated and aware of their cultural heritage. They provided the first literary criticism, and explored other aspects of myth and literature. While some created compendia of material and commentaries on older works, others created new works of literature which revisited old material in new ways. Hellenistic literature was particularly concerned with small-scale detail and the minutiae of emotional life, and with the demonstration of erudition.

The Hellenistic poet Apollonios Rhodios (Apollonius of Rhodes) gives us a very different Medea from the one we saw in Euripides' play. In his four-book epic poem the *Argonautica* Apollonios provides a narrative of the expedition to obtain the Golden Fleece, which concludes with the safe return to Iolkos. His Medea is at the beginning of her mythological journey, and he portrays her as a young, vulnerable girl overwhelmed by love for Jason. Far from being the scheming villain, Medea is presented as a victim of a terrifying attack when Aphrodite decides to make her fall in love with Jason. The assault by Eros is presented in violent, military terms:

> He [Eros] crouched down low at Jason's feet, fitted the arrow-notch to the bowstring, then stretching the bow wide in his two hands shot straight at Medea. Her spirit was seized by speechless stupor. Eros darted back out of the high-roofed palace with a mocking laugh, but his arrow burned deep in the girl's heart like a flame. (vv. 280 ff., trans. Hunter, 1993)

This refers us back to the early image of Medea in Hesiod's *Theogony* where Medea is Jason's prize. The irony of this approach comes from the self-conscious references to Euripides' story, for the great practitioner of magic falls prey to love magic herself, as Nyberg (1992) has argued. Medea struggles with her love, even after her sister Chalkiope has advised her to help Jason.

Language and rationality

Several aspects of Apollonios' presentation are interesting for our understanding of the mythology. First, he gives a great deal of attention to Medea's emotions, as a passionate young woman who tries to do the right thing. This takes us back to positive folktale patterns about the young girl who falls in love with a prince. Medea is clearly cast at this stage in the narrative as the helper-maiden who is necessary for Jason's success. However, as the narrative progresses she becomes a far more active, dominant figure, as the focus shifts from her emotional state to her magical powers.

Some have argued that in fact Medea is the hero in Apollonios' version, for it is she who is ultimately responsible for the success of the quest and the safe return home. This would provide us with an interesting take on the myth, posing the question 'Can a woman be a hero?'

An alternative reading is provided by Clauss (1997), who argues that Medea in this version is still portrayed within the dominant framework of the helper-maiden motif, specifically as a perverted version of the Nausikaa story in Homer's *Odyssey*. Clauss notes that the story motifs are inverted, as Jason wins Medea to win the Fleece, rather than the usual fairytale motivation of performing a task to win a bride. He goes on to develop a further argument drawing upon the self-conscious style of Hellenistic poetry, and argues that as the contemporary world has developed a sophisticated attitude towards myth, Jason must now become a hero in a post-mythical world. Clauss argues that there is a self-conscious technique being employed in Apollonios' story, and that a figure such as Medea can invite consideration of the nature of myth and reality. We have seen from our earliest sources that Medea posed questions about boundaries and illusion, and in the *Argonautica* we see a vivid portrayal of these issues which undoubtedly had a powerful influence on the Roman conception of Medea.

MEDEA IN ROME

Apollonios' *Argonautica* was translated into Latin hexameters by P. Terentius Varro Atacinus during the first century BC; only fragments of this poem now survive. Medea was also the subject of plays and poems by many of the leading figures of early Roman culture, such as Ennius, Pacuvius and Accius. The Hellenisation of Roman culture was highly contentious politically, as Greek culture was portrayed by some as effeminate and damaging to traditional Roman values. In this process, paradoxically, the history of Medea the barbarian became an exemplary Greek story.

Roman values shared some similarities with classical Greek ideals, but also constructed some key issues in different ways. The Roman approach to empire, for example, was to ignore cultural differences and assimilate new conquests into the Roman ideal, granting citizenship and imposing Roman institutions. As the early Roman system of republican rule was replaced by the monarchical rule of empire, many social values changed, and ideas about women, philosophy and natural processes underwent significant development. It is thus difficult to talk of a single Roman attitude towards Medea, as the Roman outlook encompasses many different historical periods, geographical areas and political structures.

Medea was a popular image for artistic representations in Rome. She is shown on a number of sarcophagi, carved burial caskets, in scenes which may relate to her liminal status as a heroine (see Schmidt, 1968). Figure 4 shows such a sarcophagus from the second century AD. The important point to note is that although such images are often referred to as 'Medea sarcophagi', Medea is not the focus of the story being told. Rather it is Kreousa (Creousa in Latin), the daughter of the king of Korinth, who is the centre of attention. The story represents an idea of untimely (and undeserved) death, which makes it appropriate for a tomb. Medea is simply the agent of this misfortune. In this scene, and those like it, we see several stages of the story: the delivery of the poison robes, on the right, followed by Kreon's doomed attempt to help his daughter as she flails around on fire, trying to get to a fountain. Medea is shown contemplating the murder of her children, and then escaping in a dragon chariot. As Kreousa is the focus, such images make Medea the sort of impersonal force of death which could take any innocent life, rather than a jealous woman killing her rival.

When Medea is shown in domestic contexts, such as the frescos in Pompeii, the interest is in her contemplation of the murder. These

Figure 4 Side of a sarcophagus depicting the legend of Medea, Roman second century (marble). Palazzo Ducale, Mantua, Italy.

Source: Image supplied by Bridgeman Art Library.

images are difficult to decode; there may have been some message about social conformity, or we may be seeing a less sophisticated use of the myth simply as a representation of Hellenised ideals. As Medea was a famous Greek figure, the pictures may have been chosen just for being 'Greek' without any close attention to their mythological significance. As we noted in Chapter 2, the accounts of myth given in visual media often raise different issues from those we confront in literary sources.

OVID

It is from the early republican period that we get our best surviving literary sources about Roman views of Medea. Ovid returned to her story several times, and may well have produced a tragedy on the subject. There are only two extant verses which, it is argued, come from this *Medea*, but there are three ancient comments (Tacitus *Dialogus* 12, Quintilian *Institutio oratoria* 8.5.6, Seneca *Suasoriae* 3.7) which suggest that Ovid's play was highly valued by his contemporaries, who viewed it as a classic of its time.

MEDEA IN *HEROIDES* 12

In *Heroides* 12, Ovid presents a tortured Medea contemplating her betrayal by Jason. There are numerous twists and turns in her thought processes, and a disjointed style of language which problematises the long traditions associating Medea with clever speech. The poem begins as if in mid sentence:

> And I remember that I, Queen of Colchis,
> found time when you came begging for help.
> Indeed, those sisters who spin the threads of life
> should have unwound at last my spindle.
> Then Medea would have ended well. But now,
> the life I live is a life of pain.
>
> (trans. Isbell, 1990)

This Medea is self-aware. She views her roles in human terms, as a source of guilt, rather than from a detached amoral divine perspective. As the poem progresses Medea jumps around from one detail of her life history to another. When she comes to tell the story of her brother's death, however, words fail her:

> But my brother, him I did not leave behind.
> My pen scratches, it cannot write on.
> What my hand did willingly, it cannot write.
> (151–3; trans. Isbell, 1990)

The contrast between word and deed is here played with to highlight the paradoxes in Medea's story. We have seen that Medea can use her voice as a weapon, to deceive or perform incantations, and yet she claims to be unable to speak of her crime. She also implies that the action was somehow easier than a vocalisation of the act. However, this is not simply a word/deed opposition. Medea does not say that she cannot 'speak' the crime, but that she cannot write it. The poem brings in sophisticated ideas about orality and literacy, perhaps suggesting that the written word has a power which Medea does not control. Such a nuanced statement about Medea's ability to articulate her views would not be out of place in the poem. At the close of the letter, Medea's revenge is set, but she expresses a perplexing awareness of her own internal chaos, concluding 'I do not know for certain what is in my soul'. Throughout the poem she has referred to numerous crimes, but she laments her weakness, speaking only of a punishment for the crime of 'too great an eagerness to trust' (v. 160). This playing with psychological self-delusion and self-knowledge can be read as a response to the sorts of philosophical and psychological issues inherent in Medea's myth which we discussed in Chapter 5.

This letter/monologue gives us an insight into Ovid's view of Medea, but the narrative account in the *Metamorphoses* contains a full life story which allows us to look once more at the connections linking the diverse elements into a single mythic biography.

MEDEA IN THE METAMORPHOSES

The epic poem was finished c. AD 7, just before Ovid's banishment. Although it contains a linear narrative, the account is far from straight-forward. It treats some episodes at length and passes over others very quickly, and does not maintain a consistent tone. There is no sustained tragic or moral stance, and we are given a range of different images of Medea and her actions. A few examples will indicate the range of approaches contained within this poem.

(a) As in the *Heroides*, Medea is given a voice at the start of Ovid's account (7. 1 ff.), but the early psychological observation is quickly lost as Medea becomes a more active figure in the story. The motif of language returns prominently at the end of the account, as Medea's ultimate fate is left unstated. She disappears from the real situation and the narrative in a clever literary conceit, literally spirited away by 'a cloud of words' (v. 424).

(b) There is a tension in the story between two opposing forces, reason and madness. *Furor*, madness or passion, is seen as a driving force at key moments, as in the opening scene (vv. 9–12):

concipit interea validos Aeëtias ignes
et luctata diu, postquam ratione furorem
vincere non poterat, 'frustra, Medea, repugnas:
nescio quis deus obstat' ait.

Meanwhile, Aeëtes' daughter harbours burning emotions;
she struggled a long time to conquer her mad passion with reason,
but finally said, 'it's useless, Medea, to fight back:
some god is against you.'

(trans. Newlands, 1997)

However, it is not simply an impersonal battle. Ovid's Medea also reflects self-consciously on her predicament, with the famous epi-grammatic line: 'video meliora proboque, deteriora sequor', 'I see the better course, and I approve of it. I follow the worse course' (7. 20–1). This injects a touch of black humour into the story which is generally missing from earlier accounts. Later centuries will use Medea as a figure of comedy, but this was generally not a part of her ancient persona.

(c) The issue of sight is very prominent in this version. Not only does Ovid indulge in elaborate, cinematic descriptions, but it is implied that his characters are as visually sensitive as his readers. When Medea is resisting her love for Jason, she takes refuge in her association with Hekate, but the sight of Jason overcomes her modesty (7. 72–3).

(d) Although Medea is the central focus and the protagonist in the story, we also see an early motif, with Medea as a trophy. Jason is described as gaining the Fleece and getting Medea as a 'second trophy', 'spolia altera' (7. 157).

Some have read Ovid's tale of Medea as irremediably disjointed: while it may be argued that the picture of Medea as the young girl displays psychological insight, there is no apparent explanation for how she becomes the child-killing witch of later sections of the story. Others have argued that for Ovid the story of Medea was simply a chance to indulge in a geographical excursus, and that the centre of interest is not Medea herself, but rather the exotic places to which she travels. However, given the fact that Ovid returned to Medea several times in his career, we should not be too quick to dismiss his interest.

Newlands's reading of the role of Medea in this poem proposes a more positive reading, contending that 'Ovid offers us not one figure, but refracted images that vary according to the different perspectives from which the reader is invited to survey them' (1997, 207). Medea is thus seen through the eyes of different characters, rather than being presented as the creation of a single authorial voice. Newlands notes the multiple images of Medea as both victim and criminal, and further emphasises the need to analyse the wider context in which Ovid presents this story. As with all the episodes in the *Metamorphoses*, the story of Medea is positioned within a wider narrative of stories within stories. Newlands points out that the other stories which frame this episode also focus on the violent acts of women, particularly in stories involving marriage. She argues that although Ovid's story does not in itself contain any explanation for Medea's crime, the surrounding tales do provide what Newlands calls 'the missing link', the explanation for why women in general act as they do.

Larmour (1990) has also argued that Ovid is creating deliberate parallels and overlaps within the *Metamorphoses*, so that the stories of Prokne and Medea are presented in similar terms. Prokne kills her child to take revenge on her husband because he raped her sister and cut out her tongue. There are, therefore, interesting thematic similarities to do with speech and silence, and the ways in which men treat women. Although the central focus of Medea's story is often taken to be the opportunity it gives Ovid for a long geographical tour, we should also note that there is thoughtful meditation on the place of Medea's story within the wider corpus of mythology.

THE METAMORPHOSIS OF MEDEA

Throughout her mythology Medea is constantly associated with transformation and metamorphosis. Her magical powers are used to change the old into the young and she herself is a chameleon, adapting to different situations. The defining moment may be the killing of Apsyrtos. The decision to help Jason is that of the young woman in love, but in order to achieve her new life as a bride Medea must act violently. But is this a change? Should we perhaps think that the 'true nature' of Medea was always the dangerous magical figure, just waiting for an opportunity?

There have been attempts to psychoanalyse Medea, as we saw in the previous chapter, and we might talk about the family dynamics of her life in Kolchis, but it is more in tune with the spirit of the mythology to look to the natural parallels. Kirke has the power to transform men into animals (and back again), and she is never presented as a tortured victim of a dysfunctional family. Metamorphosis can be seen as part of the natural process of life, as day follows night and spring follows winter. In many ways, Medea is unnatural, but as we saw in discussing previous issues, it is her exceptional position which allows us to define what is 'normal'. Medea's transformative power is particularly intriguing because it suggests not only the control of matter (as with Kirke's transformations), but also the control of time, so it is appropriate that her story is born anew into so many different contexts, and continues to live for Roman audiences, and modern audiences, just as it did in the Greek world. Medea is also an appropriate figure for detailed attention in Ovid's poem, where metamorphosis is both a theme in itself and a metaphor for various social and psychological forces.

SENECA

Seneca's tragic play *Medea* is very different from the Euripidean version. It is less subtle and more concerned with the fantastic elements of magic. Seneca is explicit about Medea's ability to raise the dead, the extreme version of her power to rejuvenate which we discussed in Chapter 4. He also gives verbatim accounts of her magic incantations, rather than preserving the mystery by giving only vague hints. His *Medea* is less complex than Euripides' version, but still contains some interesting features for the development of the myth. As we noted in Chapter 5, the Stoic background of the play allows us to read this Medea as an exemplar of the wild passions which needed to be controlled. Although she has evident supernatural powers, the expression of violent human emotions is also highlighted. Arcellaschi (1990) outlines the configuration of *Ira* (Anger), *Amor* (Love) and *Furor* (Madness/Passion) developed in the play. Traina (1979) has discussed the tension in the play between ideas of maternity and monstrosity, the positive natural force of reproduction and the negative perversion of violent destruction. Segal (1982) further notes that the name Medea is itself implicated in the process, using the alliterative force of Medea in combination with *mater*, *malum* and *monstrum*, words for 'mother' 'wickedness' and 'abomination/horror'. Combined with the Greek etymology linking her to the verb 'to plan', these factors generate a complex linguistic interplay which mirrors the mythological complexity of her character.

One further aspect of the play deserves comment. We have seen in many earlier versions that Medea is self-conscious of her own status, as if able to articulate the myth herself. In Seneca's play the culmination of the drama, when Medea decides to kill the children, is highlighted by Medea's assertion 'Medea nunc sum' (v. 910) – 'Now I am Medea'. No longer is Medea eluding definition. She is revealed as having achieved 'being' through the act of infanticide, an assertion or manifestation of her essential character or her most extreme potential. When we consider the development of the myth, the murder of the children often seems to overshadow other episodes in Medea's life, and this volume attempts to provide some corrective to this modern perception. However, in Seneca's play we appear to find confirmation that the death of the children is the defining act of Medea's life, the one episode which determines the interpretation of all others.

VALERIUS FLACCUS

The final instantiation of the Roman myth which we will consider is Valerius Flaccus' *Argonautica*, composed between AD 80 and 92. As Slavitt (1999) notes in the introduction to his translation, classicists are generally dismissive of this text, seeing it as a poor-quality, derivative poem. For our purposes, however, there are one or two interesting details. First, one of the few facts known about the author was that Valerius Flaccus was a *quindecimvir sacris faciundies*, one of the officials put in charge of the Sybilline books and the supervision of foreign cults. This suggests that he may have had access to mythological traditions which were not so well represented in mainstream literary accounts. In his poem, Medea is presented very sympathetically. She struggles against her divinely inflicted love for Jason. When Juno's first attempt fails, Venus herself is forced to get involved. It is worth noting that in the great Roman epic, Virgil's *Aeneid*, Juno is very much the villain of the piece, and that a similar attack is launched upon Dido (*Aeneid* Book 4). In the *Argonautica* Medea is presented as a figure being torn out of her world. We have seen her in other versions as a locus for the negotiation of ethnic identity, and a representation of the frightening, foreign 'other'. In this poem, Medea is made to seem a stranger in her own land, and yet the only solution, to leave, is itself shown as distressing, and Hekate is sorry to see her go. Medea herself is portrayed very much as a Roman figure, displaying expected Roman reverence towards her father (7. 309) and a sentimental attachment to animals.[1] When she puts to sleep the serpent who guards the Golden Fleece, Medea is described as feeling pity for the creature:

> Medea, seeing it helpless, ran to it, weeping tears
> for pity's sake and in shame for her own cruel behavior.
> 'Never once, in the darkest night,' she exclaimed, 'did I see you
> asleep at your post like this, when I brought you the honey-cake supper
> you nibbled out of my hand. You great, poor, hulking brute!'
>
> (8. 94 ff.; trans. Slavitt, 1999)

Medea herself is also figured mythologically as the innocent victim, as Valerius Flaccus compares her to Proserpina (5. 343–7), with the implication that she is an innocent who will be snatched away and corrupted by Jason, as Proserpina (Persephone in Greek) was snatched away by Pluto (Hades). This account of Medea is highly dependent on a number of literary predecessors, but still manages to suggest new images of Medea which can find a home in the broad church of her mythology.

OVERVIEW

In this chapter we have seen how a Greek myth concerning a quintessentially non-Greek figure could be adapted to different times, and achieve popularity in the Roman imagination. Rather than adding to the myth, the Roman versions tease out ideas and connections which are already present in the Greek accounts. The way in which Medea is transferred from Greece to Rome anticipates the way her story will find new audiences and interpreters throughout western history. In the next chapter we will examine that process, and also see how the myth finds a home in a variety of different global cultures.

AFTER GREECE AND ROME

8

MEDEA AFTERWARDS

As we have noted in previous sections, the attempt to provide a chronological narrative of the development of a myth is not necessarily useful when trying to understand the essential qualities of a mythological figure. These final chapters will not provide such a historical account, but will note key moments in the post-classical reception and comment on what the myth is doing. The previous chapter could also be considered as 'reception' material as the story moved from Greece to Rome; but as we saw, new readings of the myth also helped us to understand different aspects of the story.

PAGAN MYTHOLOGY IN A CHRISTIAN WORLD

With the coming of Christianity, the mythology of the Graeco-Roman world faced a great challenge. The pantheistic system of the Olympian gods was seen as outdated, or at worst positively evil. Temples and statues were destroyed, and the mythology which accompanied the physical remains came under threat. The survival of the stories can be attributed to a number of different factors. First, the educational traditions of the Christian church demanded that the young learn Latin and Greek, so ancient literary accounts survived as textbooks. An ability to read the languages became a mark of education and status, and many of the texts which survive from the ancient world owe their continued existence to the wealthy elite who kept personal libraries. As the story of Medea was a frequent subject in ancient literature, it stood a good chance of survival. However, the story was likely to be particularly unwelcome within the framework of Christian morality. Not only does Medea commit terrible crimes, but she is never punished for them. Some ancient stories were adaptable to Christian traditions; for instance, allegorical readings could make Heracles or Aeneas into Christlike figures. Medea was not likely to be popular in this vein. We could, however, point to the demonisation of female sexuality in early Christian thought and place Medea as an example of the need for sanctions. Saint Augustine in the late fourth century AD says that he sang 'The flying Medea' in a competition (*Confessions* 3.6.11), so clearly she was not a figure who was beyond contemplation.

Once she had survived the arrival of Christianity, Medea continued to exert a hold over the imagination of artists just as she had done in the Graeco-Roman world. The multiple meanings which could be attached to her story, and the inherent dramatic interest of such an extreme figure, gave her a role in a range of different contexts, with representations in music, dance, theatre and plastic arts. Davidson Reid (1993, 643–50) outlines an impressive number of representations involving Medea from the 1300s to the 1900s. Chaucer in the fourteenth century AD told the story of Hypsipyle and Medea in his *The Legende of Good Women*, and the resurgence of interest in the Greek world during the Renaissance ensured that the myth would remain popular. As the story of Medea acted as a fulcrum for the formation of Greek identity, she was well placed to maintain her popularity when Hellenic ideals became part of western identity.

WITCHCRAFT AND MAGIC

One of the strongest features of Medea's post-classical life is her role as the witch. We noted in Chapter 4 that magic was situated at a powerful intersection of ideas of mortality, gender and ethnicity, all issues which could well transfer to other cultures. However, it was the idea of the witch as an exotic, exciting figure which seems to have heightened Medea's popularity in some quarters. We should look to the Roman world as the strongest source of images. We can see in Shakespeare's *The Tempest* and *Macbeth* how the dramatic possibilities were exploited. Prospero's speech in *The Tempest* (Act V, lines 33 ff.) is closely modelled on Ovid's Medea in *Metamorphoses* 7, and throughout Act V there are strong parallels between Medea and the dark side of magic as represented by Sycorax, the mother of Caliban. In *Macbeth*, the violent attitude of Lady Macbeth towards her children, and her dismissal of female characteristics in favour of an 'unsexed' identity, all draw upon an image of Medea. This acts as a counterpoint to the explicit magic of the witches on the heath, who achieve their magic through the power of language and suggestion, rather than the violent action which Lady Macbeth favours.

Many artistic images emphasise Medea the witch, as in Frederick Sandys' famous painting of Medea mixing drugs in an elaborate bowl (1866–8), which hangs in the Birmingham Museum and Art Gallery. However, there are images which give a different view of Medea, as in Figure 5. This oil painting by Feuerbach comes from c. 1870 and shows Medea preparing to go into exile. At first sight this seems a pathetic, almost romantic image of the mother physically posed with her sons, but a closer examination reveals a darker side to the image. The heavy cliff face in the background, and the surf swelling around the legs of the sailors, are reminiscent of Euripides' images of Medea as heartless as water or rock. Medea herself is a static figure when compared to the sailors, and is barely holding the children, an indication of her detach-ment. Numerous details of composition indicate the darkest elements of the story (as in the mourning pose of the dark-cloaked nurse). Nevertheless, there is a strong feeling of melancholy about the scene which presents Medea more as the tragic heroine, a woman wronged, than as the dangerous cartoon character of the witch.

SOCIETY AND POLITICS

The history of images of Medea indicates changing moods in society, and interactions between literary and visual texts similar to those we saw in the Greek world. In his *Life and Death of Jason* (1867, Books 7–17) William Morris mixed a range of mythological and folkloric traditions, and presented Medea as a young pre-Raphaelite maiden who is reduced to hysterical tears by Jason's infidelity. At the same

Figure 5 'Medea preparing to go into exile.'

Source: Anselm Feuerbach, Abschied der Medea, Inv. Nr. 9826. Bayerische Staatsgemäldesammlungen, Neue Pinakothek, Munich.

time, Burne-Jones produced an image of Medea illustrating Chaucer's *The Legende of Good Women*. Although the image is pre-Raphaelite in style, there are hidden mythological links being made, as the figure is a repetition of Burne-Jones' earlier watercolour of Morgan Le Fay. Artistic considerations influence the portrayal of the figure, much as they did in the seventh century when Medea first appeared on Greek vases. The important point to note is that as modern interpreters of mythology, we may be more influenced than we realise by the images of Feuerbach, Burne-Jones et al. The 'picture which speaks a thousand words' may embed itself in our minds at a subconscious level, and may remain with us, colouring our interpretation when we look at Medea in the ancient and modern worlds.

If the artistic tradition can be powerful, but ambiguous, many of the literary versions of Medea's story were explicit attempts to place it in a contemporary context. The process of mythopoesis continued as new stories appeared, such as that of Corneille's 1635 opera in which Medea sets fire to the temple of Hera and then kills herself. A further example of this is the 1821 Austrian trilogy 'Das Golden Flieβ' of F. Grillparzar. In this account there is considerable sympathy for Medea as the abandoned wife, an account which Corti (1998) notes as having an influence over Freud: 'He clearly thought of Medea as the reasonable victim when he said in his notes "Dora: An Analysis of a Case of Hysteria", Medea is "quite content that Kreuse should make friends with her two children".' We have come a long way from the Medea of Graeco-Roman mythology and we should note that in many ways Freud was a modern mythmaker in the twentieth century, so this reading of the story is perhaps more intriguing than it at first seems. Did he really think that it was psychologically accurate that an abandoned wife would want the new woman to befriend her children?

Nineteenth-century theatrical accounts often contained sympathy for Medea, and on the English stage there were targeted productions which aired contemporary issues, related to political developments such as the Divorce Act of 1857 and the Infant Protection Act of 1872. Edith Hall (1999) has examined the ways in which the story of Medea was used as a commentary on the injustice of social legislation in England and concludes:

> The 18th Century needed to deny that Medea killed her children, or to exculpate her by a fit of madness; the 19th Century needed to change her motive from vindictive jealousy to maternal altruism. But performances of plays about Medea disappeared altogether at about the same time as the last pieces of significant Victorian marriage legislation in the early 1880s. (Hall, 1999, 70–1)

After this political association, the next direct employment of the myth comes at the turn of the nineteenth and twentieth centuries and the rise of the women's suffrage movement. In England, Gilbert Murray's translations of Greek tragedy brought myth to a wider audience, and in 1907 his translation of Euripides' *Medea* was staged at the Savoy Theatre. Medea's Corinthian speech was one of the texts used by the Actresses' Franchise League at suffragette meetings (Murray, 1913, 32), as her vengeance against an unfaithful husband was taken as a rallying call for those who believed women were being unfairly treated. Regardless of the fact that Medea in the play is a scheming murderer, her comments about the inequities of women's lives were put to use as poetic expressions of a widespread frustration. Not everyone was so inclined to forgive her violence, and a commentator on Catulle Mendes' 1898 production called Medea an example of 'the worst kind of new woman'.

INFANTICIDE – 'THE MODERN MEDEA'

One final example will indicate the complexity of the process of mythopoesis which surrounds the myth of Medea, linking myth, social unrest and artistic licence. *The Modern Medea* is the title of a painting created in nineteenth-century America by a Kentucky artist, Thomas Noble, in response to a historical event. Figure 6 shows the scene as depicted in an engraving in *Harpers' Weekly* (VII, 18 May 1867, 308). In 1865 a slave called Margaret Garner was attempting to escape with her two sons, and when caught she killed the children, by her own account, to save them from a life of slavery. The scene as shown by Noble is violent and well composed, but also shows several layers of myth making, as Weisenberger (1998) has discussed in some detail. While the immediate parallel is with a mother who kills her children,

Figure 6 'The Modern Medea: The Story of Margaret Garner.' Engraving from a painting by Thomas Noble. *Harpers' Weekly* (VII, May 18 1867, p. 308).

Source: Image supplied by The Library of Congress.

the association also implied at the time that Garner's motives were complex, that she was perhaps driven by some irrational or jealous passion, and thus distracted attention from the central issue of slavery *per se*. Assimilating Garner's story to the myth of Medea diluted the real tragic focus of her story. She became a myth and thus lost her power. We can see several issues which were present in the original myth being put to different use. The negative associations with Medea are foremost – Garner must have been (a) crazed by jealousy, (b) a witch. However, the story brings with it other associations: Medea in Euripides' version had compared marriage to slavery, and the ethnicity issue is still central. The power of myth means that those who attempt to use it for their own purposes can be caught by unanticipated implications.[1]

OVERVIEW

From the pantheistic worlds of ancient Greece and Rome, through the Christian centuries, to the political, legal debates of the nineteenth and twentieth centuries, Medea has remained a popular figure. The wide range of issues which we saw attached to her story in Chapters 3 to 5 have reappeared in different guises in different periods. The myth making has continued, and we must be alert to the role these later versions play in our own twenty-first-century attempts to understand Medea.

9

MEDEA IN THE TWENTIETH AND TWENTY-FIRST CENTURIES

In the twentieth century Medea truly came out of the domain of the educated elite. Her most powerful representations were in dramatic form, appropriately enough for a figure associated so strongly with language and disguise. Dramatised versions of Medea's story range across the world in different cultures and times, from Greece to Japan, and from Eastern Europe to South Africa and beyond. In their 2000 volume, *Medea in Performance: 1500 to 2000*, editors Hall, Macintosh and Taplin present a series of articles which testify to the wide range of productions of this one myth in English-speaking culture. Earlier publications had already explored the place of Medea in other European traditions. As there are already such good collections of information available, this final chapter will be highly selective in the items chosen for comment, not aiming for a comprehensive account, but rather looking at trends in the articulation of the myth.

POLITICAL DRAMA

The stories of Greek myth have often found a place in the language of conflict across different societies. Sophocles' *Antigone* is a frequent standard bearer for those championing the rights of the individual against the state. Many plays are used to talk about warfare and its aftermath, from the bombed-out ruins of Troy in Euripides' *Trojan*

Women to the psychological study in Simon Armitage's reworking of Euripides' *Herakles*. Armitage's play, *Mister Heracles* (2000), opens with Heracles arriving in a space suit, and examines the problem of soldiers whose violent behaviour, essential in war, proves ruinous when played out in the home.

The story of Medea has continued to be popular in the twentieth and twenty-first centuries, particularly as a commentary on political and ethnic conflict. In South Africa the social dimensions of the myth, with its examination of identity and language, have been prominent. Guy Butler's play *Demea* was written in the 1960s but only performed in the 1990s because of its political content. The play adapts the myth of Medea to a new context, setting the Jason and Medea figures as husband and wife in a mixed-race marriage. The ambiguous status of the children raises issues about colour, race and position under the unforgiving rule of apartheid. The myth continued to be relevant in the chaos which followed the collapse of the system. One production initially improvised by performers was directed by Fleishman and Reznec in several locations across South Africa between 1994 and 1996. It employed a wide range of symbols and languages to suggest the multicultural force of the story, and simultaneously to disenfranchise and disorientate all sections of the audience. No single audience member would have been able to follow all the dialogue, which ranged between a number of different languages and dialects, so everyone was put in the position of outsider. The production also made use of music, dance and ritual. Although there is a danger in comparing long-established African traditions to the ritual practices of ancient Greece (the term 'primitive' is often used in a patronising, pejorative sense) this production did emphasise the physicality of the story – killing members of one's family is a violent act, and the insult which Jason inflicts on Medea is one she feels at a physical level.

A different response to the issue of language and ethnicity can be seen in a Scottish production of Liz Lochhead's *Medea (after Euripides)*. This was a play which dispensed with divine elements, giving a greater emphasis to the human suffering and the creation of identity. Although much of the play is focused on sexual politics, Lochhead's introduction to the text of the play indicates its explicit approach to language:

it struck me that the conventional way of doing Medea in Scotland until very recently would have been to have Medea's own language Scots and the, to her, alien Corinthians she lived under speaking, as powerful 'civilised' Greeks, patrician English. That it did not occur to me to do other than give the dominant mainstream society a Scots tongue and Medea a foreigner-speaking-English refugee voice must speak of a genuine in-the-bone increased cultural confidence here. (Lochhead, 2000, unpag.)

From the violent conflicts of South Africa, to the simmering, centuries-old issues within the 'United Kingdom' the myth can be articulated to air immediate social concerns.

PERSONAL DRAMA

In Irish theatre Medea has been dramatised by prominent playwrights to a number of different ends. The political dimension of the story, particularly in Euripides' version, as an examination of imperialistic power told in the context of Anglo-Irish conflict, has attracted a number of writers, but the story has also been treated on a more personal level. Brendan Kennelly has written of how he came to the story of Medea from his own experience in a psychiatric institution. Through witnessing the conditions of women who had suffered breakdowns after relationships with abusive men, he came to the story of Medea as an example of a particular form of psychopathology, as McDonagh discusses:

His Medea is angry to the point of not caring about the long-term personal consequences of her anger, hinting at a rejection of traditional stoical acceptance of male abuse. Writing at a critical juncture in his own life, Kennelly understands Medea's anger, a vortex of self-loathing that manifests itself in the attempt to destroy all those who come close to her, culminating in the elimination of the only people who are directly of her own flesh. Perhaps she has to kill her children to stand any chance of recovering what little sanity has been afforded to her. Attempting to break the grip of alcohol, Kennelly empathises with a character that is driven to pathological unhappiness, almost relishing the darkness and chaos that typify her existence. (McDonagh, 2002, 225)

This attempt to make sense of the story proceeds in psychological rather than mythological terms, taking the action and positing an underlying pattern of causation, and yet still returns to ideas about chaos and identity which belonged to the earliest Greek instantiations of the myth. A core remains even when the myth is radically reshaped, as in Carr's play *By the Bog of Cats* (1998). The 'heroine' of this play, Hester, is an outcast, shunned because of her ethnicity and poverty. Her actions in burning her house down and killing her daughter are followed by her suicide. Although the actions themselves are not directly paralleled by the Graeco-Roman myth of Medea, they belong to the reception tradition, for Anouilh made his Medea kill herself, and such responses can be seen as ways of reframing questions central to the myth. Death in these contexts is not a mark of weakness, but a mark of strength, and Carr's Hester transcends her life in death just as Euripides' Medea escapes on a chariot.

From the origins of the Women's suffrage movement through the feminist action of the 1970s Medea has been significant as a strong female role. She has been played by outstanding actresses from Sarah Bernhardt in the late nineteenth century to Diana Rigg and Fiona Shaw in the late twentieth century. Medea has also been played in modern theatre, just as in ancient. In her analysis of Ninangawa's *Medea*, Smethurst (2000) notes the metatheatrical issue of casting Medea as a man, with the use of dolls as an indication of the actor/character's inability to bear children. Crossgender productions today also work the other way, from Fiona Shaw's portrayal of Richard II, to the Cambridge Greek Play's *Oidipous Tyrannos* of 2004, in which Oidipous and Kreon were played by women against a male Jokasta.

FILM

The twentieth century's new medium of storytelling has also seen a number of portrayals of Medea, notably versions by Pasolini (1969), Dassin (1970) and Von Trier (1988). As a medium which has transcended generic barriers and brought cultural information to a wider audience, the cinema is an important part of the modern perception of Medea. Commenting on cinematic productions, Christie (2000, 145) has gone so far as to assert that they are 'surely among the most significant twentieth-century reworkings of this mythic narrative in any medium'. Christie makes a convincing case for close study of the medium, 'reading' the myth through with all the post-structuralist tools of modern literary and dramatic analysis. Although many of the critical approaches are as much a product of our time as are the instantiations of the myth under consideration, we can also see a constant return to the themes which began in the Graeco-Roman world. The positioning of Medea as a figure of conflict between Christian and pagan worlds in Von Trier's *Medea* contains echoes of the ancient Greek problems of mortality, divinity, and the conflict between chthonic and Olympian deities which we discussed in chapter 4. It can also be read in relation to the survival of pagan myth within a Christian context which we discussed in chapter 8. Christie's comments on how Pasolini presents Medea, 'entranced' by Jason only to recover her mind in Korinth, reflect the old problem of consistency between character and narrative version which we saw from the earliest stages of the myth. Christie further highlights the different levels on which mythological thinking can operate. The closing scenes which are bathed in sunlight reflect the role of Helios as ancestor, but Christie argues that the intended meaning for Pasolini is 'apocalyptic' – the destruction of Jason and Korinth being an inevitable consequence of a decaying society.

The final film discussed by Christie, Dassin's *The Dream of Passion*, is the most metatheatrical of the three, containing a story within a story, as the tale of a 'real-life' child murderer is juxtaposed with the staging of a production of Medea. This technique immediately suggests the Ovidian technique of inset narrative and framing, which we discussed in chapter 7, but also suggests the essential self-reflexivity which Medea displays throughout her myth. We may wonder whether there is anything particularly 'twentieth-century' or 'modern' about these reworkings of the myth, or whether we are seeing the same processes played out in different forms. Analysis of the role of Medea in film can only be properly situated within a wider discussion of the changing place of the Graeco-Roman world in cinema, a topic which has received considerable attention in recent years, and the reader is

referred to the Guide to Further Reading at the back of this volume
for bibliography.

REVISIONIST READINGS

Outside the dramatic arena, there have been other approaches,
notably the revisionist reading of Christa Wolf. In her *Medea: Stimmen*
(1996) Wolf denies that Medea actually committed any crimes. It is a
version of the myth which directly confronts the ideas of patriarchy
that we discussed in chapter 4. Wolf sets the story in a world of social
change and conflict. Older, matriarchal religions, based on the power
of goddesses, are being overrun by patriarchal religions which
diminish women. The issue of power and control is linked to spiritual
problems, and the moral dilemma of how to behave when the rules of
a society are wrong. Throughout the story the mood is one of distrust
and betrayal, and Wolf conjures up an atmosphere where reality is in
question. The emphasis is not so much on magic as on how the very
idea of 'reality' is problematised in a situation where no one can be
trusted. The political dimension relates to the society of late twentieth-
century Eastern Germany, and is tied to issues of ethnic identity and
xenophobia. While it is not an overt allegory, the immediate political
context adds great resonance to the story. The extremity of Medea's
behaviour is presented as the only response to an extreme situation.

From a different perspective, Jane Cahill's (1995) account of
mythology presents Medea's stories so that her Medea is consistent:
she possesses all her attributes at one time, so that when she kills her
children it is in the knowledge that she has the power to bring them
back to life.

THE CONTINUED INTEREST OF SCHOLARSHIP

Just as Medea has continued to attract the attention of artists, so too
have classical scholars returned to her over the centuries. One reason
for this is the wide range of material and the quality of that material,
as she is a figure of lyric poetry, drama and epic. Furthermore, she is

mythologically complex, touching on many different issues. Each generation comes to her afresh and tries to make sense of her, but she is the folktale figure who changes according to fashion – the outsider, the woman scorned, the murderer, the young woman in love. In mythological terms, she is equivalent to Proteus or Thetis, who keep changing shape to evade capture. We can't pin her down, so she keeps moving and growing.

In the post-structuralist world of the late twentieth century and beyond, this chameleonic nature is welcomed. In explaining the rationale for the 1997 collection, *Medea: Essays on Medea in Myth, Literature, Philosophy and Art*, Clauss sought to explain the attraction thus: 'In confronting Medea, we confront our deepest feelings and realize that behind the delicate order we have sought to impose upon our world lurks chaos' (Clauss and Johnston, 1997, 17).

It is also the case that the increased role of women in scholarship has brought a new impetus to the study of female figures. Developments in the fields of anthropology, mythology and feminist thinking have all contributed new ways of approaching the figure of Medea. As a self-reflexive figure within a man's world Medea's story has resonances for female scholars in their own lives. Writing in 2004/2005, I am still aware that women in classical scholarship have a long way to go. The dynamics of academic hierarchies from school to university and beyond still disadvantage women. Although women on university Classical Studies courses often outnumber men, the story is different when we look at the centres of power. Boys still have greater opportunities to study ancient languages at school, and there are still far too few women at senior levels in university management. When we consider Medea's story about power and fertility, it is a sobering fact that twenty years ago maternity leave was seen as highly disadvantageous to a woman's research profile, and there is still no obvious time to have children within a traditional career structure. And yet, many men feel threatened by women and the changing gender roles we see in a modern society. Changes in employment patterns have often left men at a disadvantage and created feelings of isolation and alienation which sometimes link up to concerns about immigration and nationality. In such a world it is not surprising that Medea still holds our attention.

OVERVIEW – TIME AND PLACE

An internet search on the name 'Medea' throws up a new angle which provides a suitable point of closure for this discussion. Typing 'Medea' into different search engines one day in mid 2004 created links in at least 50 per cent of cases to the figure of Medea Benjamin, a political activist from San Francisco. What makes her name so interesting is that it is self-chosen, and has provoked some strong reactions from her opponents. Benjamin has been an outspoken critic of the Bush administration and its foreign policy, but her name change from 'Susie' to 'Medea' comes from an earlier period in her life. Her explanation has been much quoted: 'I just didn't believe the story', she said wryly of the classic tragedy. 'What woman would kill her kids for a guy? I think she was a strong woman, and some people just made up the story to discredit her.'[1]

This image of Medea as a woman treated badly by history contains echoes of the chorus in Euripides' play complaining that the poets have slandered them (see Chapter 6). However, by treating Medea as a historical figure, who can be said to have been unfairly represented, Benjamin is taking control of the myth and reshaping it in the light of her own concerns. Unfortunately, myth, as we have seen across the centuries, is a fickle servant, and Benjamin's opponents have been quick to play up the negative associations of the name.

Although it has a peculiar force, the story of Medea can only be understood within the wider context of the reception of Graeco-Roman mythology. In the introduction to *Gods and Heroes of the Greeks. The Library of Apollodorus*, Simpson talks about the role of mythology in US society in ways which we can relate to the figure of Medea Benjamin: 'I can only suggest what every aware person knows: That the turning to the study of mythology by all sorts and conditions of men and women is in part a response to the cultural fragmentation, not to say chaos, which we see all around us, and that it is one symptom, moreover, of the American social disease anomie' (Simpson, 1976, 3).

Having started this book with a warning about 'the myth of the universal', we conclude, paradoxically, with a myth of Medea referring to themes which are universal, or perhaps merely recurrent, in human society. The myth of Medea can highlight a society's views of 'the other', be they women or foreigners, followers of a different set of beliefs, or political opponents divided by ideology. We have not been able to pin her down, and perhaps that is the lesson her story is trying to teach us. We have analysed her as a figure coming from the east to the west, so now it is time to return to Kolchis. Eastern philosophies have taken a far more relaxed approach to definition and boundaries. In the so-called 'axial age' when Euripides was demystifying old stories, and Socrates was trying to reach definitions, in a different place a man who would be known as the Buddha presented a new way of seeing the world which went beyond dualistic thinking. From such a perspective Medea can be mortal *and* divine, male *and* female, a positive image of female power *and* a warning about the dangers of female passion. Instead of finding Medea puzzling as she evades our attempts to categorise her, we should perhaps be realising that every one of us is as much a perplexing composite as is Medea. We all play different roles and relate to the world in a range of different ways. The myth may compel our attention not so much because of its content as because of its process. In facing the complexities of Medea's identity we face the complexities of our own.

NOTES

I INTRODUCING MEDEA

1 The majority of names are rendered in their Greek form in this volume. The exceptions are names which are more commonly referred to in Latinised forms, particularly names of authors, so 'Aeschylus' rather than 'Aiskhylos', etc.

2 Sophocles' play does contain a reference to the Freudian structure, when Jokasta tells Oidipous not to worry 'because many men have married their mother in their dreams' (*Oidipous Tyrannos* vv. 981–2). Freudian critics would take this as evidence that there is a common psychological trait in the story. It is impossible to escape once we begin to engage with Freudian theory, because any attempt to deny a connection can be dismissed as 'denial' and thus ignored. Critics of Freud's work emphasise the immediate context in which he was writing and even later psychoanalysts who have drawn on his work have generally developed more nuanced readings. An interesting example of this is Steinem (1994), a parody of Freud's work which reverses the gender bias.

6 EURIPIDES' VERSION OF MYTH

1 The term 'metatheatre' was coined by L. Abel, *Tragedy and Metatheatre. A New View of Dramatic Form* (New York, 1963). For Abel, the term referred to theatre which highlighted the theatricality of life. It has been taken by later commentators also to refer to theatre which is self-referential, drawing attention to the artificiality of the theatrical performance.

7 MYTH ABOUT MYTH: FROM GREECE TO ROME

1 On Roman expressions of sentiments for pets see Bradley (1998).

8 MEDEA AFTER GREECE AND ROME

1 The story of Margaret Garner was the original impetus for Toni Morrison's 1987 novel *Beloved*, though Morrison has distanced herself from this, arguing that the finished novel travelled a considerable distance away from the initial spark of the idea.

9 MEDEA IN THE TWENTIETH AND TWENTY-FIRST CENTURIES

1 The quotation from 'Medea' Benjamin about her name comes from an interview recorded at http://www. sfgate.com/cgi-bin/article.cgi?file=/c/a/ 2002/10/26/MN36571.DTL.

FURTHER READING

MAJOR PRIMARY SOURCES

1. Pindar *Pythian* Ode 4, trans. in F. Nisetich, *Pindar's Victory Odes* (Baltimore, 1980).
2. Euripides' *Medea*, trans. J. M. Walton, *Euripides: Medea, Phoenician Women, Bacchae* (London, 1998).
3. Apollonios Rhodios, *Argonautica*, trans. R. Hunter, *Apollonius of Rhodes: Jason and the Golden Fleece* (Oxford, 1993).
4. Ovid, *Heroides* 12, trans. H. Isbell, *Ovid: Heroides* (London, 1990).
5. Ovid, *Metamorphoses* Book 7, trans. M. M. Innes, *Ovid: Metamorphoses* (London, 1955).
6. Seneca, *Medea*, trans. F. Ahl, *Medea* (Ithaca, 1986).
7. Valerius Flaccus, *Argonautica*, trans. D. R. Slavitt, *The Voyage of the Argo* (Baltimore, 1999).

EDITED COLLECTIONS

1. J. J. Clauss and S. I. Johnston (eds), *Medea: Essays on Medea in Myth, Literature, Philosophy and Art* (Princeton, 1997). An outstanding collection examining the figure of Medea from different angles. It contains an excellent bibliography and a useful index locorum.
2. *Pallas* 45 (1996), *Médée et la violence.* A special edition of the journal with useful articles by a number of scholars. The volume focuses on aspects of violence, from psychological interpretation to categories

of aggressive action. Summaries in English and French are provided for ease of reference.

3. B. Gentili and F. Perusino (eds), *Medea nella letteratura e nell'arte* (Venice, 2000). A collection of useful articles with some good details, but material has generally been covered elsewhere. One for advanced students, rather than the first point of call after this volume.

4. M. Schuchard and A. Speck (eds), *Medeas Wandlungen: Studien zu einem Mythos in Kunst und WissenschaftKämmerer*. Particularly useful for those interested in artistic representations of Medea, with a good bibliography.

5. *Der altsprachliche Unterricht* 40. 4–5 (1997) *Mythen Erzählen: Medea*. Journal edition containing individual articles looking at specific instantiations of the myth, including several on modern readings.

INTRODUCING MEDEA

Jung's seminal essay on archetypes is available as a separate text translated by J. Hull, *The Archetypes and the Collective Unconscious* (Princeton, 1991). See also a discussion of the relevance of archetypes to literature in M. Bodkin, *Archetypal Patterns in Poetry: Psychological Studies of Imagination* (Oxford, 1934). The anthropologist A. Lang produced three important treatises explaining his method: *Custom and Mythology* (1884), *Myth, Ritual and Religion* (1887), *The Making of Religion* (1898).

MYTHOLOGY AND SOURCES

For early sources, see T. Gantz, *Early Greek Myth: A Guide to Literary and Artistic Sources* (2 volumes) (Baltimore and London, 1993). This is a comprehensive account of the archaic and classical references to individual stories, with useful genealogical tables and detailed references to primary sources.

Braswell's commentary on Pindar *Pythian* 4 (Cambridge, 1988) gives a summary of the story of Medea from Hesiod to Pindar. An excellent detailed summary of the myth down to the time of Euripides' *Medea* is provided in Mastronarde, *Euripides: Medea* (Cambridge, 2002).

The *Lexicon Iconographicum Mythologiae Classicae* (VI. 2, 194–202) illustrates images of Medea, with a good commentary (in German) by M. Schmidt, VI.1, 386–98. There are also a number of articles which discuss the artistic tradition; see C. Sourvinou-Inwood, 'Medea at a Shifting Distance: Images and Euripidean Tragedy', in J. J. Clauss and S. I. Johnston (eds), *Medea: Essays on Medea in Myth, Literature, Philosophy and Art* (Princeton, 1997), 253–96; V. Zinserling-Paul, 'Zum Bild der Medea in der antiken Kunst', *Klio* 61 (1979), 407–36. For the interaction between mythology and religion, see S. Price and E. Kearns (eds), *The Oxford Dictionary of Classical Myth and Religion* (Oxford, 2003) – this is a good reference point for information about the basics of myth and religion, as well as comment on the latest thinking in scholarship. L. E. Doherty, *Gender and the Interpretation of Classical Myth* (London, 2001) contains a lively engagement with the theories of mythology from an explicitly feminist standpoint.

On Kallimachos' *Hekale*, see the edition of the poem, A. Hollis, *Callimachus: Hecale* (Oxford, 1990), p. 141 about the nameless 'she' who recognises Theseus on his return to Athens (fr. 232 Pfister = Hollis. fr. 4). A good survey of the approaches adopted by Hellenistic artists which may have some bearing on Apollonios' treatment can be found in B. H. Fowler, *The Hellenistic Aesthetic* (Wisconsin, 1989).

ORIGINS, FOLKTALE AND STRUCTURALISM

Folktale

The best starting point for analysis of classical myth and folklore is W. Hansen, *Ariadne's Thread: A Guide to International Tales Found in Classical Literature* (Ithaca and London, 2002). For the idea of the helper-maiden motif and its relationship to gendered readings of myth, see Doherty, *Gender and the Interpretation of Classical Myth*. For the motif of child-killing see J. Fontenrose, 'The Sorrows of Ino and Procne', *TAPA* 79 (1948), 125–67. Thought-provoking comment on gendered readings of story can also be found in M. Warner, *From the Beast to the Blonde: On Fairy Tales and Their Tellers* (New York, 1995).

Structuralism

The seminal article by Lévi-Strauss is 'The Structural Study of Myth', *Journal of American Folklore* 68. 270 (1955). For the contributions made by Lévi-Strauss and others to this debate, see M. Hénaff (trans. Mary Baker), *Claude Lévi-Strauss and the Making of Structural Anthropology* (London and Minneapolis, 1998).

WITCHCRAFT, CHILDREN AND DIVINITY

Witchcraft

There are several good surveys of magic in the ancient world. The best starting point is D. Ogden, *Magic, Witchcraft and Ghosts in the Greek and Roman Worlds: A Sourcebook* (Oxford, 2002). This is a comprehensive account of witchcraft, providing major sources in translation plus commentary and contextualisation. Chapter 5 focuses on Medea and Circe. See also M. W. Dickie, *Magic and Magicians in the Graeco-Roman World* (London, 2001); V. Flint, R. Gordon, G. Luck and D. Ogden, *The Athlone History of Witchcraft and Magic in Europe: Volume 2, Ancient Greece and Rome* (London, 1999); for analysis of the role of magic in literature, see H. Parry, *Thelxis: Magic and Imagination in Greek Myth and Poetry* (Lanham, MD, 1992).

On magic see M. W. Dickie, 'Talos Bewitched: Magic, Atomic Theory and Paradoxography in Apollonius' *Argonautica* 4. 1638–88', *Papers of the Leeds International Latin Seminar* 6 (1990), 267–96 – a detailed analysis of the scientific and psychological ideas which lie behind Apollonios' account. See also J. J. Winkler, 'The Constraints of Desire: Erotic Magic Spells', in *The Constraints of Desire: The Anthropology of Sex and Gender in Ancient Greece* (London and New York, 1990). For the evidence of the practice of cursing in the ancient world, see J. G. Gager, *Curse Tablets and Binding Spells from the Ancient World*

(Oxford, 1992); H. D. Betz, *The Greek Magical Papyri in Translation, Including the Demotic Spells* (2nd edn, Chicago, 1992).

On Theocritus' *Idyll* 2 and the interaction between poetry and magic, see F. T. Griffiths, 'Poetry as Pharmakon in Theocritus Idyll 2', in G. W. Bowerstock, W. Burkert and M. J. Putnam, *Arktouros: Hellenic Studies Presented to Bernard M. W. Knox on the Occasion of his Sixty-Fifth Birthday* (Berlin), 81–8. On Medea herself as a *pharmakis*, see M. Belloni, 'Medea πολυφαρμακος', *CCC* 2 (1981), 117–33. For those interested in the historical interpretation of witches, see D. Purkiss, *The Witch in History. Early Modern and Twentieth Century Presentations* (London and New York, 1996). This is not a catalogue, but an analysis of the interaction of texts and the use of the witch figure for particular purposes. Excellent analysis of the witch in drama, with some comment on the use of ancient sources.

Children

See P. E. Easterling, 'The Infanticide in Euripides' *Medea*', *Yale Classical Studies* 25 (1977), 77–91. In this influential article Easterling analysed the Euripidean version in the light of recently reported incidents in which mothers kill their own children. More recently, Sztulman has argued that Medea's loss of family is related to a psychological breakdown: H. Sztulman, 'Le mythique, le tragique, le psychique: Médée. De la deception à la dépression et au passage a l'acte infanticide chez un sujet état-limite', *Pallas* 45 (1996), 46–74. See also L. Corti, *The Myth of Medea and the Murder of Children* (Westport, CT, 1998). This is an idiosyncratic reading of the myth, which understands the story as related to psychological trauma and society's hostility towards children.

On the problems of ancient exposure of children, see M. Golden, 'Did the Ancients Care When their Children Died?', *Greece and Rome* 35 (1988), 152–63. For discussion of the vase showing Medea and Herakles, see M. Schmidt, 'Medea und Herakles, zwei tragische Kindermörder', in E. Böhr and W. Martini (eds), *Studien zur Mythologie und Vasenmalerei* (Mainz am Rhein, 1986), 169–74. For further thoughts from this volume's author about Herakles and ideas of mortality, see E. M. Griffiths, 'Euripides' *Herakles* and the Pursuit of Immortality', *Mnemosyne* 52 (2002), 641–56. On Mesopotamian myths of child-killing demons, see J. A. Scurlock, 'Baby-Snatching Demons, Restless Souls and the Dangers of Childbirth: Medico-Magical Means of Dealing with Some of the Perils of Motherhood in Ancient Mesopotamia', *Incognita* 2 (1991), 1–112.

Divinity

For a good survey of the practices of Greek religion, see S. Price, *Religions of the Ancient Greeks* (Cambridge, 1999). On the interplay between magic and religion, see R. Fowler, 'Greek Magic, Greek Religion', *Illinois Classical Studies* 20 (1995), 1–22. On Hekate, see D. Boedeker, 'Hecate: A Transfunctional Goddess in the *Theogony*?', *TAPA* 113 (1983), 79–97.

ETHNICITY, GENDER AND PHILOSOPHY

Ethnic identity

On the general principles of 'Them and Us' in Greek thought, see P. Cartledge, *The Greeks. A Portrait of Self and Others* (Oxford, 1993), a very good introduction to the principles of self-definition by concepts of 'the Other'. A related text, examining ethnicity in Greek tragedy, is E. Hall, *Inventing the Barbarian: Greek Self-Definition through Tragedy* (Oxford, 1989). For the details of Pericles' citizenship law, see A. Boegehold, 'Perikles' Citizenship Law of 451/0 BC', in A. Boegehold and A. Scafuro (eds), *Athenian Identity and Civic Ideology* (Cambridge, 1994), 57–66, and on the links between this law and Euripides' play, R. Friedrich, 'Medea Apolis: On Euripides' Dramatization of the Crisis of the Polis', in A. H. Sommerstein et al. (eds), *Tragedy, Comedy and the Polis* (Bari, 1993), 219–39. The use of the witch figure as a locus of ethnic definition is well discussed in Chapter 10 of D. Purkiss, *The Witch in History. Early Modern and Twentieth Century Presentations* (London and New York, 1996).

Gender

For a general overview of the position of women in Greece, see N. Demand, *Birth, Death and Motherhood in Classical Greece* (Baltimore, 1994). For ideas about sexuality and gender in Greece see D. M. Halperin, J. J. Winkler and F. I. Zeitlin (eds), *Before Sexuality: The Construction of Erotic Experience in the Ancient Greek World* (Princeton, 1990). The issues raised by women's voices, not only in drama, are well discussed by M. McClure, *Spoken Like a Woman. Speech and Gender in Athenian Drama* (Princeton, 1999). See also, G. Holst-Warhaft, *Dangerous Voices: Women's Laments and Greek Literature* (London, 1992), for an exploration of the ways in which lamentation gave women a voice in society. The power of language wielded by Kirke and Medea is discussed by H. Parry, 'Circe and the Poets: Theocritus IX 35–36', *Illinois Classical Studies* 12.1 (1987), 7–22. On the status of drama as 'other' and, therefore, feminine, the seminal article is F. I. Zeitlin, 'Playing the Other. Theater, Theatricality and the Feminine in Greek Drama', in J. J. Winkler and F. I. Zeitlin (eds), *Nothing to do with Dionysos?* (Princeton, 1990), 63–96.

Philosophy

The status of the scholarly debate about the possible interpolation in Euripides can be judged from Mastronarde's commentary (2002, Appendix pp. 386 ff.). The philosophical readings of Medea are well discussed by J. M. Dillon, 'Medea among the Philosophers', in J. J. Clauss and S. I. Johnston (eds), *Medea: Essays on Medea in Myth, Literature, Philosophy and Art* (Princeton, 1997), 211–18. See also C. Gill, 'Two Monologues of Self-Division: Euripides' *Medea* 1021–80 and Seneca's *Medea* 893–977', in P. Hardie and M. Whitby (eds), *Homo Viator: Classical Essays for John Bramble* (Bristol, 1987), 25–37. A piece more orientated towards philosophers than the general audience is C. Gill, 'Did Chrysippus Understand Medea?', *Phronesis* 28 (1983), 136–49.

EURIPIDES

The best starting point (after reading the play itself!) is W. Allen, *Euripides: Medea* (London, 2002), a short introduction which outlines the main themes of the play and its reception. The best commentary on the Greek text is D. Mastronarde, *Euripides: Medea* (Cambridge, 2002). This is suitable for those learning Greek and those at a more advanced level, and is also useful for those reading the text in translation. A long introduction outlines the progression of the myth before Euripides and includes a clear summary of the possible relationship between Euripides' play and Neophron's. Those reading the play in Greek might also like to see A. F. Elliott, *Euripides: Medea* (Oxford, 1969), a short but useful commentary designed to give linguistic help. For a helpful account of the surviving details of fragmentary and lost plays see T. B. L. Webster, *The Tragedies of Euripides* (London, 1967). A good account of the role of Medea in lost Greek plays can be found in M. Bell'do, 'Les autres Médées du théatre grec', in *Pallas* 45 (1996), 57–69. See also, D. Pralon, 'Les Peliades d'Euripide', in *Pallas* 45 (1996), 69–86.

A good survey of the evidence for and against the presence of women in fifth-century audiences of drama is given in A. J. Podlecki, 'Could Women Attend the Theater in Ancient Athens?', *Ancient World* 21 (1990), 27–43. See also, S. Goldhill, 'Representing Democracy: Women at the Great Dionysia', in R. Osborne and S. Hornblower (eds), *Ritual, Finance, Politics* (Oxford, 1994), 349–69.

The idea that Medea destroys her femininity when she kills her children is argued by several scholars, including L. Galis, 'Medea's Metamorphosis', *Eranos* 90 (1992), 65–81, and A. P. Burnett, 'Medea and the Tragedy of Revenge', *Classical Philology* 68.1 (1973), 1–24.

GREECE TO ROME

The popularity of Greek drama in southern Italy is well discussed by W. Allan, 'Euripides in Megale Hellas. Some Aspects of the Early Reception of Tragedy', *Greece and Rome* 48 (2001), 67–80. For the role of Medea in Apollonios' *Argonautica* see R. L. Hunter, *Argonautica, Book III* (Cambridge, 1989).

The role of Medea in the artistic tradition from Greece to Rome is discussed in U. Reinhardt, 'Die Kindermörderin im Bild. Beispiele aus der Kunsttradition als Erzänzung literarischer Texte zum Medea-mythos', in B. Gentili and F. Perusino (eds), *Medea nella letteratura e nell'arte* (Venice, 2000), 89–106.

Discussion of the role of Medea on Roman sarcophagi can be found in Chapter 2 of P. Zanker and B. C. Ewald, *Mit Mythen Leben. Die Bilderwelt der römischen Sarkophage* (Munich, 2004). See also M. Schmidt, *Der Basler Medeasarkophag* (Tübingen, 1968).The appearances of Medea in early Latin drama are discussed by A. Arcellaschi, *Médée dans le théâtre latin d'Ennius à Sénèque* (Rome, 1990). On Ovid's Medea see S. Hinds, 'Medea in Ovid: Scenes from the Life of an Intertextual Heroine', *Materiali e Discussioni* 30 (1993), 9–47; C. Newlands, 'The Metamorphosis of Ovid's Medea', in J. J. Clauss and S. I. Johnston (eds), *Medea: Essays on Medea in Myth, Literature, Philosophy and Art* (Princeton, 1997), 178–210. In the same volume, see on Seneca's Medea M. Nussbaum, 'Serpents in the Soul: A Reading of Seneca's Medea'. On Senecan tragedy generally, two readings which see Medea the character as dramaturge are M. Erasmo, *Roman Tragedy. Theatre and Theatricality* (Austin, 2004); T. Boyle, *Tragic Seneca* (London, 1997). For the role of Medea in Valerius Flaccus' *Argonautica*, see T. Stover, 'Confronting Medea: Genre, Gender and Allusion in the *Argonautica* of Valerius Flaccus', *CPh* 98.2 (2003), 123–47.

AFTER GREECE AND ROME

For the relationship between Seneca and Shakespeare see B. Arkins, 'Heavy Seneca: His Influence on Shakespeare's Tragedies', *Classics Ireland*, 2 (1995).

For those interested in dramatic representations, the best place to start is E. Hall, F. Macintosh and O. Taplin (eds), *Medea in Performance: 1500–2000* (Oxford, 2000). The focus is on theatrical performances in the English-speaking world but it provides a useful starting point for literature on the wider global traditions, especially in Greece and Japan. See also, E. Hall, 'Medea and British Legislation before the First World War', *Greece and Rome* n.s. 46 (1999), 42–77. This article presents an analysis of the use of the myth to speak of topical political concerns, especially the issue of divorce.

MEDEA IN THE TWENTIETH AND TWENTY-FIRST CENTURIES

Liz Lochhead's play is published as L. Lochhead, *Medea (after Euripides)* (London, 2000). On the South African experiences of Medea, see M. Mezzabotta, 'Ancient Greek Drama in the New South Africa', in L. Hardwick et al. (eds), *Theatre: Ancient and Modern* (Milton Keynes, 2000).

There has been considerable scholarship about Medea in the cinema, a mainly European phenomenon: G. Iérano, 'Tre Medee del Novecento: Alvaro, Pasolin, Wolf', in B. Gentili and F. Perusino (eds), *Medea nella letteratura e nell'arte* (Venice, 2000), 177–98; B. Feichtinger, 'Medeas sehen. Pier Paolo Pasolinis Film "Medea" im Unterricht', in *Der altsprachliche Unterricht* 40. 4–5 (1997), *Mythen Erzählen: Medea*, 107–19; D. N. Mimoso Ruiz, 'Le myth de Médée au cinéma: l'incandescence de la violence à l'image', in *Pallas* 45 (1996), *Médée et la violence*, 251–68; C. Wolf, *Medea: Stimmen* (Darmstadt, 1996), translated into English as J. Cullen, *Medea: A Modern Retelling* (London, 1998). A reading of this work which emphasises the East German context is U. Schmidt-Berger, 'Christa Wolf's "Medea". Eine feministische Transformation des Mythos', in *Der altsprachliche Unterricht* 40. 4–5 (1997) *Mythen Erzählen: Medea*, 127–40.

For the issue of women's roles in classical scholarship see, for example, the personal view of V. Zajko, 'False Things which Seem Like the Truth', in J. P. Hallett and T. Van Nortwick (eds), *Compromising Traditions: The Personal Voice in Classical Scholarship* (London and New York, 1997), 54–72.

WORKS CITED

Aldrete, C. S. (1999), *Gestures and Exclamations in Ancient Rome* (Baltimore and London).

Allan, W. (2001), 'Euripides in Megale Hellas. Some Aspects of the Early Reception of Tragedy', *Greece and Rome* 48: 67–86.

Arcellaschi, A. (1990) *Médée dans le théâtre latin d'Ennius à Sénèque* (Rome).

Barry, M. (1996), *Beginning Theory* (Manchester).

Belloni, L. (1981), 'Medea πολυφαρμακος', *CCC* 2: 117–33.

Bernabé, A. (1987), *Poetae Epici Graeci 1* (Leipzig).

Betz, H. D. (1992), *The Greek Magical Papyri in Translation, including the Demotic Spells* (2nd edn, Chicago).

Boardman, J. (1965), *The Greeks Overseas. The Early Colonies and Trade* (London).

Bodkin, M. (1934), *Archetypal Patterns in Poetry: Pyschological Studies of Imagination* (Oxford).

Boedeker, D. (1983), 'Hecate: A Transfunctional Goddess in the *Theogony*?', *TAPA* 113: 79–101.

—— (1997), 'Becoming Medea: Assimilation in Euripides', in J. J. Clauss and S. I. Johnston (eds), *Medea: Essays on Medea in Myth, Literature, Philosophy and Art* (Princeton), 127–48.

Boegehold, A. (1994), 'Perikles' Citizenship Law of 451/0 BC', in A. Boegehold and A. Scafuro (eds), *Athenian Identity and Civic Ideology* (Cambridge), 57–66.

Bradley, K. (1998), 'The Sentimental Education of the Roman Child. The Role of Pet-Keeping', *Latomus* 57: 523–57.

Braswell, K. (1988), *Commentary on Pindar Pythian Ode 4* (Cambridge).

Bremmer, J. N. and Horsfall, N. M. (1987), *Roman Myth and Mythography* (BICS supplement) (London).

Burnett, A. (1971), *Catastrophe Survived: Euripides' Plays of Mixed Reversal* (Oxford).

—— (1973), '*Medea* and the Tragedy of Revenge', *CPh* 68: 1–24.

Butler, J. (1990), *Gender Trouble: Feminism and the Subversion of Identity* (London).

Cahill, J. (1995), *Her Kind: Stories of Women from Greek Mythology* (Orchard Park, NY).

Carpenter, T. H. (1991), *Art and Myth in Ancient Greece* (London).

Cartledge, P. (1993), *The Greeks. A Portrait of Self and Others* (Oxford).

Christie, I. (2000), 'Between Magic and Realism: Medea on Film', in E. Hall, F. Macintosh and O. Taplin (eds), *Medea 1500–2000* (Oxford), 142–67.

Clauss, J. J. (1997), 'Conquest of the Mephistophelian Nausicaa: Medea's Role in Apollonius' Redefinition of the Epic Hero', in J. J. Clauss and S. I. Johnston (eds), *Medea: Essays on Medea in Myth, Literature, Philosophy and Art* (Princeton), 149–77.

Clauss, J. J. and Johnston, S. I. (eds) (1997), *Medea: Essays on Medea in Myth, Literature, Philosophy and Art* (Princeton).

Collins, D. (2003), 'Nature, Cause and Agency in Greek Magic', *TAPA* 13.1: 17–50.

Corti, L. (1998), *The Myth of Medea and the Murder of Children* (Westport, CT).

Cyrino, M. (1996), 'When Grief is Pain. The Psychodynamics of Abandonment and Filicide in Euripides' *Medea*', *Pacific Coast Philology* 3: 1–12.

Davidson Reid, J. (1993) 'Medea', in *Oxford Guide to Classical Mythology in the Arts 1300–1900s* (Oxford), 643–50.

Davies, M. (1989), 'Deianeira and Medea: A Footnote to the Pre-History of Two Myths', *Mnemosyne* 42: 469–72.

Des Places, E. (1971), *Oracles Chaldaïques, Avec un choix de commentaries anciens* (Paris).

Dickie, M. W. (1990), 'Talos Bewitched: Magic, Atomic Theory and Paradoxography in Apollonius' *Argonautica* 4. 1638–88', *Papers of the Leeds International Latin Seminar* 6: 267–96.

—— (2000), 'Who Practised Love-Magic in Classical Antiquity and in the Late Roman World?', *CQ* 50: 563–8.

Dillon, J. M. (1990), 'Medea among the Philosophers', in J. J. Clauss and S. I. Johnston (eds), *Medea: Essays on Medea in Myth, Literature, Philosophy and Art* (Princeton), 211–18.

Doherty, L. E. (2001), *Gender and the Interpretation of Classical Myth* (London).

Dowden, K. (1989), *Death and the Maiden. Girls' Initiation Rites in Greek Mythology* (London).

Dunn, F. M. (1994), 'Euripides and the Rites of Hera Akraia', *GRBS* 35: 103–15.

Easterling, P. E. (1977), 'The Infanticide in Euripides' *Medea*', *Yale Classical Studies* 25: 77–91.

Eisner, R. (1979), 'Euripides' Use of Myth', *Arethusa* 121: 153–74.

Elliott, A. F. (1969), *Euripides: Medea* (Oxford).

Erasmo, M. (2004), *Roman Tragedy. Theatre and Theatricality* (Austin).

Evans, J. G. and Jones, R. M. (eds) (1973) *Llyr Gwyn Rhydderch* (Cardiff).

Falivene, M. R. (2000), 'L'invincible debolezza: Medea nella Argonautica di Apollonio Rodio', in B. Gentili and F. Perusino (eds), *Medea nella letteratura e nell'arte* (Venice), 109–16.

Friedrich, R. (1993), 'Medea Apolis: On Euripides' Dramatization of the Crisis of the Polis', in A. H. Sommerstein *et al.* (eds), *Tragedy, Comedy and the Polis* (Bari), 219–39.

Fontenrose, J. (1948), 'The Sorrows of Ino and Procne', *TAPA* 79: 125–67.

Fowler, B. H. (1990), *The Hellenistic Aesthetic* (Madison, WI).

Fowler, R. (1995), 'Greek Magic, Greek Religion', *Illinois Classical Studies* 20: 1–22.

Frazer, J. (1922), *The Golden Bough* (abr., London, 1993).

Gager, J. G. (1992), *Curse Tablets and Binding Spells from the Ancient World* (Oxford).

Gantz, T. (1993), *Early Greek Myth: A Guide to Literary and Artistic Sources* (2 volumes) (Baltimore and London).

Gentili, B. and Perusino, F. (eds) (2000), *Medea nella letteratura e nell'arte* (Venice).

Giannini, P. (2000), 'Medea nell'epica e nella poesia lirica e tardo arcaica', in B. Gentili and F. Perusino (eds), *Medea nella letteratura e nell'arte* (Venice), 65–82.

Gill, C. (1983), 'Did Chrysippus Understand Medea?', *Phronesis* 28: 136–49.

—— (1987) 'Two Monologues of Self-Division: Euripides' *Medea* 1021–80 and Seneca's *Medea* 893–977', in M. Whitby, P. Hardie and M. Whitby (eds), *Homo Viator: Classical Essays for John Bramble* (Bristol), 25–37.

Golden, M. (1988), 'Did the Ancients Care when their Children Died?' *Greece and Rome* 35: 152–63.

Graf, F. (1997), 'Medea: The Enchantress from Afar. Remarks on a Well-Known Myth', in J. J. Clauss and S. I. Johnston (eds), *Medea: Essays on Medea in Myth, Literature, Philosophy and Art* (Princeton), 21–43.

Griffiths, E. M. (2002), 'Euripides' *Herakles* and the Pursuit of Immortality', *Mnemosyne* 52: 641–56.

Griffiths, F. T. (1979), 'Poetry as Pharmakon in Theocritus Idyll 2', in G. W. Bowerstock, W. Burkert and M. J. Putnam (eds), *Arktouros: Hellenic Studies presented to Bernard M. W. Knox on the Occasion of his Sixty-Fifth Birthday* (Berlin), 81–8.

Guirard, H. (1996), 'La Figure de Médée sur les vases grecs', *Pallas 45, Médée et la violence*, 207–18.

Gummert, P. (1997), 'Medea in des *Argonautica* des Apollonios Rhodios', in *Der altsprachliche Unterricht* 40. 4–5, *Mythen Erzählen: Medea*, 5–15.

Gutzwiller, K. (2004), 'Seeing Thought: Timomachus' Medea and the Ecphrastic Epigram', *AJPh* 125: 339–86.

Hall, E. (1989), *Inventing the Barbarian: Greek Self-Definition through Tragedy* (Oxford).

—— (1999), 'Medea and British Legislation before the First World War', *Greece and Rome* 46: 42–77.

Halm-Tisserant, M. (1993), *Cannibalisme et immortalité* (Paris).

Hansen, W. (2002), *Ariadne's Thread: A Guide to International Tales Found in Classical Literature* (Ithaca and London).

Hard, R. (1997), *Apollodorus: The Library of Greek Mythology* (Oxford).

Hénaff, M. (1998) (trans. Mary Baker) *Claude Lévi-Strauss and the Making of Structural Anthropology* (London and Minneapolis).

Hesk, J. P. (2000), *Deception and Democracy in Classical Athens* (Cambridge).

Hinds, S. (1993), 'Medea in Ovid: Scenes from the Life of an Intertextual Heroine', *Materiali e Discussioni* 30: 9–47.

Hoffer, P. C. and Hull, N. E. H. (1984), *Murdering Mothers: Infanticide in England and New England 1558–1803* (New York and London).

Holland, L. (2003), 'Myth and Plot in Euripides' *Medea*', *TAPA* 133.2: 255–80.

Holst-Warhaft, G. (1992), *Dangerous Voices: Women's Laments and Greek Literature* (London).

Hunter, R. (1989), *Argonautica Book III* (Cambridge).

—— (1993), *Apollonius of Rhodes: Jason and the Golden Fleece* (Oxford).

Hutchinson, G. (1988), *Hellenistic Poetry* (Oxford).

Huxley, G. (1969), *Greek Epic Poetry from Eumelos to Panyassis* (London).

Johnston, S. I. (1990), *Hekate Soteira: A Study of Hekate's Roles in the Chaldean Oracles and Related Literature* (Atlanta, GA).

—— (1995) 'Defining the Dreadful: Remarks on the Greek Child-Killing Demon', in P. Mirecki and M. Meyer (eds), *Ancient Magic and Ritual Power* (Leiden), 355–81.

—— (1997) 'Corinthian Medea and the Cult of Hera Akraia', in J. J. Clauss and S. I. Johnston (eds), *Medea: Essays on Medea in Myth, Literature, Philosophy and Art* (Princeton), 44–70.

—— (1999), *Restless Dead. Encounters Between the Living and the Dead in Ancient Greece* (Berkeley).

Isbell, H. (trans.) (1990), *Ovid: Heroides* (New York).

Isler-Kerényi, M. (2000), 'Immagini di Medea', in B. Gentili and F. Perusino (eds), *Medea nella letteratura e nell'arte* (Venice), 117–38.

Jackson-Knight, W. F. (1970), *Elysion. Ancient Greek and Roman Beliefs concerning Life after Death* (London).

Jones, G. and Jones, T. (1949), *The Mabinogion* (London).

Jung, C. G. (1991), *The Archetypes and the Collective Unconscious* (trans. R. F. C. Hull) (London).

Just, R. (1989), *Women in Athenian Law and Life* (London).

Kestner, J. (1989), *Mythology and Misogyny: The Social Discourse of Nineteenth-Century British Classical-Subject Painting* (Madison, WI).

King, H. (1998), *Hippocrates' Women: Reading the Female Body in Ancient Greece* (London and New York).

Knox, B. M. (1977), 'The *Medea* of Euripides', *Yale Classical Studies* 25: 193–225.

Kovacs, D. (1986), 'On Medea's Great Monologue (Eur. Medea 1021–80)', *CQ* 36: 343–52.

—— (1993) 'Zeus in Euripides' Medea', *AJPh* 114: 45–70.

Lada-Richards, I. (1999), *Initiating Dionysus. Ritual and Theatre in Aristophanes' Frogs* (Oxford).

Lang, A. (1884), *Custom and Mythology*.

—— (1887), *Myth, Ritual and Religion*.

—— (1898), *The Making of Religion*.

Larmour, D. H. J. (1990), 'Tragic Contaminatio in Ovid's Metamorphoses: Procne and Medea; Philomela and Iphigeneia (6.424–74); Scylla and Phaedra (8.19–151)', *Illinois Classical Studies* 15.1: 131–41.

Larson, J. (1995), *Greek Heroine Cults* (Madison, WI).

Lesky, A. (1931), 'Medeia', *RE* 15: 29–65.

Lévi-Strauss, C. (1955), 'The Structural Study of Myth', *American Journal of Folklore*.

Lloyd, G. E. R. (1979), *Magic, Reason and Experience: Studies in the Origin and Development of Greek Science* (Cambridge).

Lochhead, L. (2000), *Medea (after Euripides)* (London).

Loraux, N. (1995), *The Experiences of Tiresias: The Feminine and the Greek Man* (Princeton).

Lyons, D. (1997), *Gender and Immortality. Heroines in Ancient Greek Myth and Cult* (Princeton).

Mackie, C. J. (2001), 'The Earliest Jason: What's in a Name?', *Greece and Rome* 48: 102–23.

Maitland, J. (1992), 'Dynasty and Family in the Athenian City-State: A View from Attic Tragedy', *CQ* n.s. 42: 26–40.

Martindale, C. (1993), *Redeeming the Text: Latin Poetry and the Hermeneutics of Reception* (Cambridge).

—— (1997), 'Proper Voices: Writing the Writer', in J. P. Hallett and T. Van Nortwick (eds), *Compromising Traditions: The Personal Voice in Classical Scholarship* (London and New York), 71–101.

Mastronarde, D. M. (ed.) (2002), *Euripides: Medea* (Cambridge).

McClure L. (1999), *Spoken Like a Woman. Speech and Gender in Athenian Drama* (Princeton).

McDermott, E. A. (1989), *Euripides' Medea: The Incarnation of Disorder* (University Park, PA).

McDonagh, J. (2002), 'Is Medea's Crime Medea's Glory? Euripides in Dublin', in M. McDonald and J. M. Walton (eds), *Amid Our Troubles: Irish Versions of Greek Tragedy* (London), 213–31.

McGinty, P. (1978), *Interpretation and Dionysos* (The Hague).

Melville, A. D. (trans.) (1986) *Ovid: Metamorphoses* (Oxford).

Michelini, A. N. (1987), *Euripides and the Tragic Tradition* (Madison, WI).

Mimosa-Ruiz, D. (1982), *Médée antique et moderne. Aspects rituals et socio-politiques d'un mythe* (Paris).

Moreau, A. (1994), *Le Mythe de Jason et Médée: La va-nu-pied et la sorcière* (Paris).

Morris, W. (1867), *The Life and Death of Jason* (London).

Murray, G. (1913), *The Medea of Euripides* (London).

Newlands, C. (1997), 'The Metamorphosis of Ovid's Medea', in J. J. Clauss and S. I. Johnston (eds), *Medea: Essays on Medea in Myth, Literature, Philosophy and Art* (Princeton), 178–208.

Newman, J. K. (2001), 'Euripides' *Medea*: Structures of Estrangement', *Illinois Classical Studies* 26: 53–76.

Nikolaidis, A. G. (1985), 'Some Observations on Ovid's Lost Medea', *Latomus* 44: 383–7.

Nisetich, F. (1980), *Pindar's Victory Odes* (Baltimore).

Nyberg, L. (1992), *Unity and Coherence: Studies in Apollonius Rhodius' Argonautica and the Alexandrian Epic Tradition* (Lund).

O'Brian, J. V. (1993), *The Transformation of Hera: A Study of Ritual, Hero and the Goddess in the 'Iliad'* (Lanham, MD).

Orwin, T. (1994), *The Humanity of Thucydides* (Princeton).

Page, D. L. (1938), *Euripides: Medea* (Oxford).

Parry, H. (1987), 'Circe and the Poets: Theocritus IX 35–36', *Illinois Classical Studies* 12.1: 7–22.

—— (1988), 'Magic and the Songstress. Theocritus *Idyll* 2', *Illinois Classical Studies* 13.1: 1–24.

Pentikaïnen, J. (1968), *The Nordic Dead-Child Tradition. A Study in Comparative Religion* (Helsinki).

Price, S. (1999), *Religions of the Ancient Greeks* (Cambridge).

Purkiss, D. (1996), *The Witch in History: Early Modern and Twentieth-Century Representations* (London).

Rabinowitz, N. and Richlin, A. (eds) (1993), *Feminist Theory and the Classics* (New York and London).

Radermacher, L. (1943), *Mythos und Sage bei den Griechen* (Vienna).

Reinhardt, U. (2000), 'Die Kindermörderin im Bild. Beispiele aus der Kunsttradition als Erzänzung literarischer Texte zum Medea-mythos', in B. Gentili and F. Perusino (eds), *Medea nella letteratura e nell'arte* (Venice), 89–106.

Rickert, G. (1987), 'Akrasia and Euripides' Medea', *Harvard Studies in Classical Philology* 91: 91–117.

Schmidt, M. (1968), *Der Basler Medeasarkophag* (Tübingen).

—— (1986), 'Medea und Herakles, zwei tragische Kindermörder', in E. Böhr and W. Martini (eds), *Studien zur Mythologie und Vasenmalerei* (Mainz am Rhein), 169–74.

Scurlock, J. A. (1991), 'Baby-Snatching Demons, Restless Souls and the Dangers of Childbirth: Medico-Magical Means of Dealing with Some of the Perils of Motherhood in Ancient Mesopotamia', *Incognita* 2: 1–112.

Seaford, R. (1994), *Ritual and Reciprocity: Homer and Tragedy in the Developing City-Stage* (Oxford).

Seidensticker, B. (1990), 'Euripides, *Medea* 1056–80: An Interpolation?' in M. Griffith and D.J. Mastronarde (eds), *Cabinet of the Muses* (Atlanta), 89–102.

Segal, C. P. (1982), 'Nomen sacrum. Mede and other names in Senecan tragedy', *Maia* n.s. 34: 241–6.

Seznec, J. (1953), *The Survival of the Pagan Gods: The Mythological Tradition and its Place in Renaissance Humanism and Art* (New York).

Sfyroeras, P. (1994), 'The Aigeus Scene in Euripides' *Medea*', *CJ* 90: 125–42.

Simpson, B. (1976), *Gods and Heroes of the Greeks. The Library of Apollodorus.* (Amherst).

Slavitt, D. (trans.) (1999), *The Voyage of the Argo: The Argonautica of Gaius Valerius Flaccus* (Baltimore).

Smethurst, M. (2000), 'The Japanese Presence in Ninagawa's *Medea*', in E. Hall, F. Macintosh and O. Taplin (eds), *Medea in Performance 1500–2000* (Oxford), 191–216.

Smith, C. (1999), 'Medea in Italy: Trade and Contact between Greece and Italy in the Archaic Period', in G. R. Tsetkhladze (ed.), *Ancient Greeks West and East* (Leiden), 123–45.

Sourvinou-Inwood, C. (1991), *'Reading' Greek Culture* (Oxford).

—— (1995), *'Reading' Greek Death* (Oxford).

—— (1997), 'Medea at a Shifting Distance. Images and Euripidean Tragedy', in J. J. Clauss and S. I. Johnston (eds), *Medea: Essays on Medea in Myth, Literature, Philosophy and Art* (Princeton), 242–70.

Steinem, G. (1994), 'What if Freud were Phyllis?', in G. Steinem, *Moving Beyond Words* (London), 32–90.

Stone, D. (1984), 'Medea and Imitation in the French Renaissance', *Illinois Classical Studies* 9: 215–28.

Stover, T. (2003), 'Confronting Medea: Genre, Gender and Allusion in the *Argonautica* of Valerius Flaccus', *CPh* 98.2: 12–47.

Stowell, S. (1992), *A Stage of their Own. Feminist Playwrights of the Suffrage Era* (Manchester).

Sztulman, H. (1996), 'Le Mythique, le tragique, le psychique: Médée. De la deception à la dépression et au passage a l'acte infanticide chez un sujet état-limite', in *Pallas* 45: 45–67.

Traina, A. (1979), 'Due note a Seneca tragico', *Maia* 31: 273–6.

Thompson, S. (1961), *The Types of the Folktale: A Classification and Bibliography. Antti Aarne's Verzeichnis de Märchentypen (FF Communication no. 3) translated and enlarged by S. Thompson* (2nd edn, Helsinki).

Turner, F. W. (1989), 'Why the Greeks and not the Romans in Victorian Britain?', in G. W. Clarke (ed.), *Rediscovering Hellenism: The Hellenic Inheritance and the English Imagination* (Cambridge), 61–81.

Visser, M. (1986), 'Medea: Daughter, Sister, Wife and Mother. Natal Family versus Conjugal Family in Greek and Roman Myths about Women', in M. Cropp, E. Fantham and S. Scully (eds), *Greek Tragedy and its Legacy. Studies presented to D. J. Conacher* (Calgary), 149–65.

Walton, J. M. and Thompson, D. (2000), *Euripides: Medea, The Phoenician Women, Bacchae* (London).

Warner, M. (1995), *From the Beast to the Blonde: On Fairy Tales and Their Tellers* (New York).

Weisenberger, S. (1998), *'Modern Medea': A Family Story of Slavery and Child-Murder from the Old South* (New York).

West, M. (1966), *Hesiod: Theogony* (Oxford).

—— (1971), *Iambi et Elegi Graeci* (Oxford).

Will, E. (1955), *Korinthiaka* (Paris).

Winkler, J. J. (1990), 'The Constraints of Desire: Erotic Magic Spells', in J. J. Winkler (ed.), *The Constraints of Desire: The Anthropology of Sex and Gender in Ancient Greece* (London and New York), 12–34.

—— (2001) (ed.), *Classical Myth and Culture in the Cinema* (Oxford).

Winter, C. (1960), *Hekate: Studien zu Wesen und Bild der Göttin in Kleinasien und Griechenland* (Heidelberg).

Zajko, V. (1997), 'False Things which Seem Like the Truth', in J. P. Hallett and T. Van Nortwick (eds), *Compromising Traditions: The Personal Voice in Classical Scholarship* (London and New York), 54–72.

Zeitlin, F. I. (1990), 'Playing the Other. Theater, Theatricality and the Feminine in Greek Drama', in J. J. Winkler and F. I. Zeitlin (eds), *Nothing to do with Dionysos?* (Princeton), 63–96.

Zerba, M. (2002), 'Medea Hypokrites', *Arethusa* 35: 315–37.

Zinserling-Paul, V. (1979), 'Zum Bild der Medea in der antiken Kunst', *Klio* 61: 407–36.

INDEX

witch, witchcraft 41–2, 46–7, 57–8,
    60, 104–5
women, as actors 64; fear of 47,
    68; and female bonds 62; good
    woman/bad woman 67, 79;
    and identity 62; inferior mental
    powers of 69; intelligence of
    74; and lamentation 64; male
    understanding of 66; as 'other'
    61; and scholarship 117;

secondary position of 63; as
    storytellers 37; violence of 95;
    as vulnerable/weak 62, 73,
    see also feminism; gender
Women's Suffrage Movement
    114

Zerba, M. 64, 80
Zeus 15, 31, 54, 62, 76, 88
Zeus Horkios 76

Related titles from Routledge

Prometheus

Carol Dougherty

Myths and legends of this rebellious god, who defied Zeus to steal fire for mankind, thrive in art and literature from ancient Greece to the present day. Prometheus' gifts to mortals of the raw materials of culture and technological advancement, along with the curse of despair that followed the enlightenment of humankind, have formed the basis of a poetic and powerful embodiment of the human condition.

Seeking to locate the nature of this compelling tale's continuing relevance throughout history, Carol Dougherty traces a history of the myth from its origins in ancient Greece to its resurgence in the works of the Romantic age and beyond. A Prometheus emerges that was a rebel against Zeus's tyranny to Aeschylus, a defender of political and artistic integrity to Shelley and a symbol of technological innovation during the industrial revolution, his resilience and adaptability illuminating his power and importance in Western culture.

This book provides a comprehensive introduction to the Prometheus myth, emphasising the vitality and flexibility of his myth in a variety of historical, literary, and artistic contexts of the ancient Greeks, the Romantics, and twentieth-century English poet, Tony Harrison. It is an essential introduction to the Promethean myth for readers interested in Classics, the arts and literature alike.

Hb: 0–415–32405–X
Pb: 0–415–32406–8

Available at all good bookshops
For ordering and further information please visit:
www.routledge.com

Related titles from Routledge

Zeus

Ken Dowden

Sovereign ruler of the universe, controller of the weather, all-seeing father of gods and men: Zeus was the chief deity of the ancient Greek pantheon. His places of worship ranged from the household to Olympia, the greatest of all sanctuaries. His significance is reflected in the many chapters dedicated to him in books on Greek religion and myth but this is the first attempt to capture him in the round, in a single volume, for many years.

In a study that is at once masterly and comprehensive, Ken Dowden presents a study of this fascinating god for the new millennium. Myth, cult, art and art are examined, as are philosophy, drama, theology, European painting and much more. Not only is the period of the ancient Greeks covered but that of their predecessors, and above all that of their successors, the Romans. The importance of Zeus in the medieval period and modern times is discussed in a revealing section on reception.

The book contains many and varied illustrations, charts and maps and provides a thorough and accessible, as well as scholarly, introduction to the chief god in the Greek pantheon.

Hb: 0–415–30502–0
Pb: 0–415–30503–9

Related titles from Routledge

Greek Mysteries

The Archaeology of Ancient Greek Secret Cults

Edited by Michael B. Cosmopoulos

Religion in ancient Greece had a strong public character and was, in many respects, a way of integrating the individual into the community. Within this public religion, there were special cults – 'mysteries'. These were selected voluntarily by each person in the polis, allowing them to deal with the gods on an individual basis. Privacy was needed for the practice of the mysteries, and this was secured by an initiation ceremony that brought each person to a new spiritual level, and a higher degree of awareness in relation to the gods.

With the lack of written evidence that exists for the mysteries, archaeology has proved central to explaining their significance, and this welcome volume showcases new research on the archaeology, ritual and history of Greek mystery cults. Contributions range through Greece and Greek Asia Minor, and from the Bronze Age to the Roman imperial period. While the main focus is on major sites such as Eleusis and Samothrace, a conscious effort has been made to incorporate the large number of lesser known mysteric cults and deities.

Written by an international team of acknowledged experts, *Greek Mysteries* makes an important contribution to understanding a phenomenon central to Greek religion and society.

Hb: 0–415–24872–8
Pb: 0–415–24873–6

Available at all good bookshops
For ordering and further information please visit:
www.routledge.com